9 0 2

Complete Course in English Book 2

A NEW REVISED EDITION

D1564056

Robert J. Dixson

In collaboration with
J. Andújar

 Prentice Hall Regents, Englewood Cliffs, NJ 07632

Photo editor: Robert Sietsema
Cover design: Paul Gamarello
Text design: Judy Allan, The Designing Woman

Printed in the United States of America

10 9 8 7 6

ISBN   0-13-158825-7

Prentice-Hall International (UK) Limited, *London*
Prentice-Hall of Australia Pty. Limited, *Sydney*
Prentice-Hall Canada Inc., *Toronto*
Prentice-Hall Hispanoamericana, S.A., *Mexico*
Prentice-Hall of India Private Limited, *New Delhi*
Prentice-Hall of Japan, Inc., *Tokyo*
Simon & Schuster Asia Pte. Ltd., *Singapore*
Editora Prentice-Hall do Brasil, Ltda., *Rio de Janeiro*

foreword

The revised editions of the four books of *Complete Course in English* make up a practical course stressing the conversational forms and everyday vocabulary of spoken American English. Each unit includes ample oral practice and encourages students to take an active role in their learning.

The texts are designed to be adaptable to a wide variety of teaching techniques. We suggest, however, that the teacher start each period with a review of the previous session's work before beginning a new lesson. Because the text introduces new grammar and new speech patterns at a steady rate, no more than one lesson should be covered in any session. The class should maintain a schedule of constant review and repetition, and should not proceed to a new lesson until students have first demonstrated oral mastery of the current lesson.

Teachers should encourage students to learn full-form (complete sentence) patterns but also to learn and practice the more common, contracted-form patterns for use in their conversational English.

In Book 2, Units 10 and 22 are reviews of the vocabulary and grammar covered up to those points. Each of the other twenty units has four parts: a dialogue, a grammar and usage section, an exercise section, and a reading and conversation section. The dialogue represents either a typical conversation which could take place between native speakers of American English or a short story which usually includes a brief conversation within it. This section also presents the points of grammar and usage introduced in the unit in a natural, conversational way. Following this section there are ten questions about the dialogue or story. These questions will help the teacher test for comprehension and stimulate some conversation about the subject of the dialogue or story.

The grammar and usage and exercise sections provide practice with important principles of grammar. A brief explanation is first given of the grammatical point in question; then some examples are provided. There follows next a series of simple exercises covering the point. Teachers may supplement these exercises by offering additional oral drills wherever possible. Oral drills and practice are important if a student is to be able to carry over the knowledge of the point and incorporate it into his or her everyday speech.

The reading and conversation sections contain a reading selection followed by a series of questions about the selection. Included also are questions designed to stimulate conversation and to expand on the subject of the reading. Following the questions are lists of the new words which have been introduced in the unit along with some special phrases for further vocabulary study. Teachers should use ingenuity to expand on the questions in the text and in the study of the vocabulary words and phrases, directing the students into conversational channels.

The final part of each unit is a pronunciation drill which introduces all the important sounds of English. Teachers should have their students repeat the sounds both chorally and individually while guiding them and correcting errors in pronunciation.

contents

Complete Course in English

Robert Sietsema

unit one

Dialogue

MS. BARRA: Hi, Elaine.

HAIRDRESSER: Hello, Ms. Barra. I'll be with you in a minute. *(a few minutes later)* Now, what do you want to do with your hair today?

MS. BARRA: I'm tired of having long hair. Please cut it a lot shorter this time.

HAIRDRESSER: Oh, your hair isn't *that* long. Look at the pictures in this book and see if you really like the short styles. *(a few minutes later)* Come this way and I'll give you a wash.

MS. BARRA: Don't use your regular shampoo; use a gentle one, please.

HAIRDRESSER: Do you want a little coloring today, also?

MS. BARRA: No, I'm happy with it like this. Well, on second thought, perhaps you can put on a little tint to cover the gray. But don't put on too much!

HAIRDRESSER: I won't. Now let's see which styles in this book would look good on you.

MS. BARRA: I think I like this one. It would be easy to take care of.

HAIRDRESSER: Let's do it!

Answer these questions:
1. Where does this dialogue take place?
2. What does Ms. Barra want Elaine to do?
3. What does Elaine give her to look at?
4. What is shampoo? How do you use it? What kind do you use?
5. Why does Elaine want to wash Ms. Barra's hair first?
6. How many times a week do you wash your hair?
7. Does Ms. Barra want to change the color of her hair?

8. Why do people change the color of their hair? Would you like to change the color of your hair?
9. What color is your hair? What color do you think Ms. Barra's hair is?
10. What does Ms. Barra decide to do?

Grammar and Usage

1. The Imperative Form

a. The imperative form expresses a command or request. To form the imperative in English, we use the infinitive without *to*. There is only one form for singular and plural. The subject (you) is understood but not expressed.
Wait here!
Go with him.

b. We form the negative of the imperative with *do not* (usually contracted to *don't*).
Don't wait here.
Don't go with him.

c. To form the first person plural of the imperative, we use *let us* (usually contracted to *let's*) followed by the infinitive without *to*.
Let's eat in that restaurant.
Let's not eat in that restaurant.

2. Some/any

We use *some* in affirmative sentences. We use *any* in negative sentences and in questions.
He has *some* friends in Chicago.
He doesn't have *any* friends in Chicago.
Does he have *any* friends in Chicago.

Exercises

A. Change these sentences first to the negative form then to questions. Make the appropriate change from *some* to *any*.

1. I made some mistakes on my last test. (I didn't make *any* mistakes on my last test. Did I make *any* mistakes on my last test?)
2. There were some bottles of ammonia on that counter.
3. He made some speeches during the summer.
4. She mispronounced some of the words in the dialogue.
5. There are some drugstores in that shopping center.
6. We have some new neighbors.
7. They removed some stones from the road.
8. There are some students from Nigeria in this class.

B. Change these sentences to the imperative form.
   1. You may come back later. (Come back later.)
   2. You should wait for me on the corner.
   3. You may use a contraction in that sentence.
   4. You girls should sit in these chairs.
   5. You can leave the room.
   6. You will eat your sandwich.
   7. You can hide behind that tree.
   8. You students should be quiet.

C. Change the following affirmative sentences to negative ones.
   1. Come back later. (Don't come back later.)
   2. Wait for me after school today.
   3. Call her on the phone tonight.
   4. Help them move that stone from the middle of the road.
   5. Hide in the other room.
   6. Ask him to go to the movies with us.
   7. Tell the teacher what we are doing.
   8. Give him your phone number.

D. Change these sentences to the first person plural, imperative form. Use the contracted form.
   1. Go to the theater. (Let's go to the theater.)
   2. Ask Dolores to go with us.
   3. Buy a newspaper.
   4. Start the engine of the car.
   5. Help him move those stones from the middle of the road.
   6. Go to the restaurant around the corner.

7. Tell the teacher we like this exercise.
8. Finish this exercise.

Reading and Conversation:
The Stone in the Road

Many years ago, there lived a very rich man who wanted to do something for the people of his town. But first he wanted to find out whether they deserved his help. So he placed a very large stone in the center of the main road into town. Then he hid behind a tree and waited. Soon an old man came along with his cow.

"Who put this stone in the center of the road?" said the old man, but he did not try to remove the stone. Instead, with some difficulty he passed around the stone and continued on his way. Another man came along and did the same thing; then another came, and another. All of them complained about the stone in the center of the road, but not one of them tried to remove it. Late in the afternoon, a young man came along. He saw the stone and said, "The night will be very dark. Some neighbor will come along later in the dark and will fall against the stone."

The young man then began to move the stone. He pushed and pulled with all his strength to move it to one side. But imagine his surprise when under the stone he found a bag full of money and this message: "This money is for the thoughtful person who removes this stone from the road. That person deserves help."

A. Comprehension and Conversation

1. Why did the rich man place the stone in the road?
2. Who passed by first? What did he do?
3. Where was the rich man while the people passed by?
4. What did the young man who passed by in the evening do when he saw the stone?
5. What kind of young man was he?
6. What did he find under the stone?
7. What would you do if you saw a large stone blocking your path?

8. Why do you think all the other people complained but did not move the stone?
9. Have you ever found any money? What did you do with it?
10. Do you think this is a true story? Why/Why not? Did you enjoy it?

B. Vocabulary

Nouns		*Verbs*		*Other*
style	middle	do (something) for	hide	rich
ammonia аммиак	theater	look good	find out	main
shampoo	engine	deserve заслуживать	remove	perhaps
hair	center	choose	complain	behind
shopping	cow	look through	push	instead
center	road	put on	pull	
neighbor	strength		imagine	
block	surprise			
stone	bag			
sandwich				

C. Expressions

Use each of these expressions in a sentence.
on second thought, with some difficulty, at first, at last, on his way.

D. Pronunciation Drill

ŋ   as in sang, tongue, longing

sing	laughing	hungry
bring	coming	English
ring	going	language
long	making	stronger
thing	doing	younger
wing	waiting	angry

New York Convention and Visitors Bureau

unit two

Dialogue

STUDENT: I hear that you are going to New York for the holidays, Ms. Nash.

TEACHER: Yes, I am going to leave on Thursday.

STUDENT: How long are you going to be there?

TEACHER: I'll be in New York for about ten days. I'm planning to get back here the day before school opens.

STUDENT: What are you going to do while you're in New York?

TEACHER: I am going mainly to see my family. They live in New York.

STUDENT: But aren't you going to go to any shows or restaurants while you're there?

TEACHER: I may have dinner with a few friends and go to the movies once or twice, but that's about all. I'm not going to spend much money on my trip.

STUDENT: Why not?

TEACHER: Because I don't have much. I'm not going by plane, for example, because it costs too much.

STUDENT: I thought you were going to fly.

TEACHER: I was going to fly, but then I saw the price of the tickets.

STUDENT: How are you going to get there?

TEACHER: Believe it or not, I'm going by bus.

Answer these questions:
1. Where is Ms. Nash going for the holidays? When?
2. How long is she going to be there?
3. What is she going to do while she's there?
4. Why isn't she going to spend much money while she's in New York?
5. How was she going to get there?
6. Why did she change her mind?
7. How is she going to get there?
8. What are the main holidays in your country?

9. Where are you going on your next vacation?
10. What were you planning to do last weekend? Did you do it?

Grammar and Usage

The *Going to* Future Tense

a. In modern English, when we wish to express simple future action or the intention to do something in the future, we use the phrase *to be going to,* followed by the infinitive.* We use *shall* and *will* in the future only to express promise or determination.

Singular	*Plural*
I am going to work	we are going to work
you are going to work	you are going to work
he	
she is going to work	they are going to work
it	

The contracted form:

Singular	*Plural*
I'm going to work	we're going to work
you're going to work	you're going to work
he's	
she's going to work	they're going to work
it's	

b. We form the negative of the *going to* future by placing *not* after *to be.*
    I am going to work.
       I am *not* going to work. (I'm not going . . .)
    He is going to swim.
       He is *not* going to swim. (He's not going . . .)

c. We form the question of the *going to* future by placing *to be* in front of the subject.
    We are going to arrive at six.
    Are we going to arrive at six?
    When *are* we going to arrive?
    You are going to see a movie.

---

* Compare this with the use of *ir* in Spanish and Portuguese.

Are you going to see a movie?
What *are* you going to see?

d. If we wish to use the verb *to go* together with the phrase *to be going to,* as in the sentence "He is going to go to New York next week," we usually shorten the sentence to "He is going to New York next week."

I *am going to* the movies tomorrow night.
He *is going* to Chicago with us next week.

e. We use the past form of *to be going to* to describe an action which was planned but did not happen.*

We *were going to* play tennis yesterday, but it rained.
I *was going to* telephone you, but I could not find your number.

Exercises

A. Supply the *going to* future in the blanks.
1. He is going to visit us next week. (visit)
2. They _____ to Los Angeles. (move)
3. I _____ this exercise correctly. (do)
4. There _____ a new movie at the Strand this week. (be)
5. We _____ to Caracas next week. (fly)
6. You _____ this question correctly. (answer)
7. She _____ to the drugstore. (go)
8. It _____ tomorrow. (rain)

B. Change these sentences first to negative form then to questions. Use contractions where possible.
1. She is going to do her homework. (She's not going to do her homework. Is she going to do her homework?)
2. It's going to be cold tonight.
3. I'm going to the art museum this afternoon.
4. We're going to eat at a restaurant tonight.
5. He's going to go to a nightclub in Lima.
6. There's going to be a good show on TV tonight.

---

* Compare this with the use of the past tense of *ir* in Spanish and Portuguese.

7. They are going to call us in the morning.
8. You are going to hide behind that tree.

C. Change the following so as to use the past form of the *going to* future.
   1. I wanted to go to Rome, but I couldn't afford it. (I was going to go to Rome, but I couldn't afford it.)
   2. She wanted to tell him, but she didn't have time.
   3. He wanted to see that movie, but he didn't.
   4. They wanted to fly, but they went by train instead.
   5. I wanted to call you, but I didn't have your number.
   6. We wanted to study last night, but some friends came over to visit.
   7. I wanted to lend you my book, but I lost it.
   8. The cat wanted to come in, but the door was locked.

Reading and Conversation: Progress

Peter's father wanted to know how his son was getting along in school. One day he asked him, "Peter, how are you getting along in school? What is your rank among the students?"

"I'm number twenty-one, Dad. The teacher seats us according to our marks. I'm in the twenty-first seat."

"And how many students are there in your class?"

"Twenty-one."

Several weeks passed. Peter was not a good student; he never studied for his examinations. One day he came home with his report card.

"How are you getting along in school now, Peter?" his father asked. "Your grades do not seem to be very good."

"I'm getting along a little better now, Dad."

"What is your rank in the class now?"

"Twenty. I'm in the twentieth seat."

"Good. That means you moved up one place."

"Well, not really. One of the students left the class. His family moved to another town."

A. Comprehension and Conversation

1. What did Peter's father want to know?
2. What did he ask his son?

3. Do your parents ask you how you are getting along in school?
4. How are you getting along in school?
5. In your classes, how is your seat chosen?
6. How many students are there in Peter's class? What was his rank in the class?
7. How many students are there in your English class? What is your rank?
8. Do you get good grades on your English examinations?
9. How do we know that Peter was not a good student?
10. What do you think Peter's father will do now?

B. Vocabulary

Nouns		Verbs	Other
holiday	show	afford	once
nightclub	grade	borrow	twice
price	art museum	get along	correctly
drugstore		rank	mainly
		seem	according to

C. Expressions

Use each of these expressions in a sentence.
the day before, for example, believe it or not, change your mind.

D. Pronunciation Drill

h   as in <u>h</u>at, be<u>h</u>ind, <u>wh</u>ole

heat	him	behind
have	her	perhaps
hat	hide	anyhow
help	his	behave
hear	who	unhappy
hello	how	ahead

Robert Sietsema

unit three

Dialogue

NANCY:	Hello, I'm calling for someone named Asher. I don't know the first name.
MR. NOVAK:	We don't have anyone here by that name.
NANCY:	Isn't this 555-3109?
MR. NOVAK:	No, this is 555-3119. You have the wrong number.
NANCY:	I'm sorry. I must have misdialed. *(She dials again.)*
MR. ASHER:	Hello, Ted Asher speaking. Is there something I can do for you?
NANCY:	I don't know. I have a message to call a Mr. Asher.
MR. ASHER:	Doesn't your message say anything else?
NANCY:	No. It's a mystery to me. You said your name is Asher. Don't you know why you called me?
MR. ASHER:	What's your name?
NANCY:	Nancy Petridis.
MR. ASHER:	I'm sorry, I don't know anyone by that name. I wish I could help you, but I don't know anything about this.
NANCY:	Can't you think of any reason why you might have left a message for me?
MR. ASHER:	No, I'm sorry.
NANCY:	I wish someone would help us solve this mystery.
MR. ASHER:	So do I.

Answer these questions:
1. Whom was Nancy calling? What happened on her first call?
2. What number did she dial? What number did she want to dial?
3. Do you sometimes call a wrong number? What do you usually say when you find out it's the wrong number?

4. Is it easy for you to remember phone numbers? Do you often have to look up people's numbers?
5. Is your telephone number in the phone book?
6. What happened when Nancy finally reached Mr. Asher?
7. What was the mystery of this short dialogue?
8. How did Nancy try to solve the mystery?
9. Do you make many phone calls each week? How many?
10. Do you like to talk on the telephone? Which people do you like to talk to?

Grammar and Usage

1. *Someone/anyone; something/anything*

We learned that we use *some* in affirmative sentences and *any* in negative sentences and in questions. Similarly, words derived from *some,* such as *somebody, someone, something,* and *somewhere,* are used in affirmative sentences. Words derived from *any,* such as *anybody, anyone, anything,* and *anywhere,* are used in negative sentences and in questions.

There is *someone* in the room.
There isn't *anyone* in the room.
Is there *anyone* in the room?
He gave them *something* to eat.
He didn't give them *anything* to eat.
Did he give them *anything* to eat?

2. Negative Questions

We form negative questions in the same way that we form regular questions, by placing the auxiliary verb before the subject. In conversational English, we almost always use contracted forms in negative questions.

He didn't go with them.
Didn't he go with them?
She doesn't study with them.
Doesn't she study with them?
They can't come today.
Can't they come today?

Exercises

A. Change these sentences to the negative form.
   1. There's someone at the door. (There isn't anyone at the door.)
   2. There's somebody in your office.
   3. She'll bring someone with her.
   4. He gave me something to read.
   5. I found my book somewhere in your house.
   6. You left something on the desk.
   7. It was something important.
   8. He said something about a meeting.

B. Change these sentences to questions.
   1. She went somewhere with him last night. (Did she go anywhere with him last night?)
   2. You found something in his office.
   3. He saw someone in the room.
   4. There is someone waiting for you.
   5. She lost something.
   6. She went somewhere last night with her boyfriend.
   7. You told somebody about it.
   8. There was somebody at the door when you called.

C. Change these sentences to negative questions using contractions.
   1. He didn't want to buy the book. (Didn't he want to buy the book?)
   2. She doesn't like to get up early.
   3. You don't like to speak in front of a lot of people.
   4. We can't study in your class.
   5. You couldn't come to class yesterday.
   6. It won't rain tomorrow.
   7. It isn't time to leave.
   8. There won't be any buses today.

D. Change these sentences to questions beginning with *why*.
   1. He doesn't study in our class. (Why doesn't he study in our class?)
   2. You didn't leave a message for me.
   3. The bus doesn't stop at this corner.
   4. You couldn't wait for me.

5. We won't be in school tomorrow.
6. They don't like the house they live in.
7. She doesn't want to use her father's car.
8. She doesn't know the name of my teacher.

Reading and Conversation: A Joke on a Friend

Mark Twain was a famous American writer. He wrote many famous stories which are still popular in many countries today. Twain was also famous in his day as a public speaker. In his speeches, Twain always liked to tell funny stories. He also liked to listen to funny stories and to play jokes on his friends. One day, one of Mark Twain's friends lost his wallet and asked Mark Twain to pay his train fare for him.

"But I don't have enough money to pay both your fare and my fare," Mark Twain said. The friend did not know what to do. He was very sad. "We can do this," said Mark Twain. "We can get on the train and, when the conductor comes to take the tickets, you can hide under my seat."

However, when the conductor came to take the tickets, Twain gave him two tickets—one for himself and one for his friend. Then, in a loud voice, Mark Twain explained, "My friend here is a very strange man. When he travels on a train, he does not like to sit on the seat. He prefers to lie on the floor under the seat."

Of course, everybody in the train then looked at the poor friend under the seat and laughed at him loudly.

A. Comprehension and Conversation

1. Who was Mark Twain?
2. What happened to his friend? What did his friend ask Twain to do?
3. What was Twain's answer?
4. What plan did Twain suggest?
5. What happened when the conductor came through the train?
6. What joke did Mark Twain then play on his friend?
7. Do you like to play jokes on your friends? Give an example of a joke that you played on a friend.

8. Do you like it when people play jokes on you? Give an example of a joke that someone played on you.
9. What would you do if you lost your wallet after you got on a train?
10. Do you think you would laugh if you saw a trick like the one in the story?

B. Vocabulary

Nouns	*Verbs*		*Adjectives*
message	dial	lie	popular
mystery	misdial	sit	loud
reason	solve		sad
wallet	remember		strange
boyfriend	look up		poor
joke	reach		public
conductor	explain		

C. Expressions

Use each of these expressions in a sentence.
wrong number, I'm sorry, play a joke, public speaker.

D. Pronunciation Drill

θ   as in thin, author, health

thank	Thursday	both	mathematician
thing	thirty	method	south
think	three	birthday	north
through	thought	cloth	thirtieth

Mexican Government Tourism Office

unit four

Dialogue

RUTH: Can you guess where I'm from? It's the largest city in the United States.

PABLO: Washington, D.C.?

RUTH: No, Washington is the capital, but it's not the largest city. New York is the largest city in the United States.

PABLO: I thought Washington was larger than New York.

RUTH: No, Washington is smaller than New York. Washington is also smaller than Chicago and Los Angeles, but it's larger than Boston.

PABLO: I come from the most beautiful city in Mexico. My city is Guadalajara. Many people disagree, but I believe it is more beautiful than Mexico City.

RUTH: Is Guadalajara also the most interesting city in your country?

PABLO: No, Mexico City is more interesting than Guadalajara. There is more to do in Mexico City.

RUTH: Is Guadalajara larger than Mexico City?

PABLO: No, Guadalajara is smaller than Mexico City. Mexico City is the largest city in Mexico.

Answer these questions:
1. What is the capital of the United States? What is the capital of your country?
2. What is the largest city in the United States?
3. What is the largest city in your country? Is it larger than New York? Is it larger than Mexico City?
4. What is the most interesting city in your country? The most beautiful?
5. What is the tallest building in your city?

6. Who is the tallest person in your family? Who is the shortest?
7. Who is the most popular writer in your country? Is he or she more famous than Mark Twain?
8. Is Washington, D.C., larger than Boston? Than Los Angeles?
9. Is Guadalajara larger than Mexico City? Than New York?
10. What is the easiest language to learn? The hardest?

Grammar and Usage

1. The Comparative and Superlative Forms of Adjectives

a. For adjectives of one syllable and some adjectives of two syllables, we form the comparative by adding -er. We form the superlative by adding -est.

	Comparative	Superlative
old	older	oldest
small	smaller	smallest
happy	happier	happiest
easy	easier	easiest

b. For adjectives having more than two syllables and some adjectives of two syllables, we form the comparative with *more* and the superlative with *most*.

	Comparative	Superlative
beautiful	more beautiful	most beautiful
interesting	more interesting	most interesting
careful	more careful	most careful
clever	more clever	most clever

c. A few adjectives have special comparative and superlative forms.

	Comparative	Superlative
good	better	best
bad	worse	worst

	Comparative	*Superlative*
little	less	least
many	more	most

d. The comparative form of adjectives is always followed by *than*.
   Washington is smaller *than* New York.
   She is more famous *than* her sister.

2. A Special Use of Infinitives

a. When verbs such as *tell, ask, want,* and *order* are used to express a wish or a command, they are followed by an infinitive. Note that the subject of the infinitive is in the objective case.
   The director told *us to come* back later.
   She asked *me to wait* for her.

b. The negative of this construction is formed by placing *not* before the infinitive.
   The director told us *not* to come back later.
   She asked me *not* to wait for her.

Exercises

A. Supply the comparative form of the adjective in parentheses.
   1. Guadalajara is a more beautiful city than Mexico City. (beautiful)
   2. New York is _____ Chicago. (large)
   3. This book is _____ that one. (expensive)
   4. The weather today is _____ the weather yesterday. (warm)
   5. These pears are _____ those. (good)
   6. He is a _____ student _____ his brother. (bad)
   7. These exercises are _____ the other ones. (difficult)
   8. Are you _____ your sister? (tall)

B. Supply the superlative form of the adjective in parentheses.
1. Guadalajara is the <u>most beautiful</u> city in Mexico. (beautiful)
2. Alice is the _____ girl in our class. (tall)
3. Carlos is the _____ boy in his class. (smart)
4. He is the _____ student in class. (good)
5. This book is the _____ one that I have. (expensive)
6. Andrea wears the _____ clothes of anyone in this room. (interesting)
7. The Mark Twain story is the _____ in the book. (funny)
8. This is the _____ pencil in the box. (bad)

C. Change the adjective in each sentence to the comparative form. Add whatever words are necessary to complete the meaning.
1. Carlos is a good student. (Carlos is a better student than his brother.)
2. This is a warm day.
3. She is an intelligent student.
4. This is an expensive book.
5. This is an easy exercise.
6. This restaurant is crowded.
7. We had many ideas.
8. I am a strong person.

D. Repeat Exercise C, changing the adjectives to the superlative form. Add whatever words are necessary to complete the meaning.
1. Carlos is a good student. (Carlos is the best student in the class.)

E. Fill in the blanks with one of the following objective case pronouns: *me, you, him, her, it, us, them.*
1. He asked <u>me</u> to wait for him.
2. Jerry told _____ to come back later.
3. Nancy asked _____ to go for a walk with her.
4. The teacher ordered _____ to sit down.
5. He wanted _____ to go to the party with him.

6. They told _____ to wake them up at seven o'clock.
7. The police officer ordered _____ to put his hands up.
8. We wanted _____ to rain.

F. Change the following sentences to negatives by placing *not* before the infinitive.
   1. She asked me go to. (She asked me not to go.)
   2. Mark Twain told him to sit next to him.
   3. They asked us to wake them before noon.
   4. He told us to wait on the corner for him.
   5. She asked him to tell her friend about it.
   6. I asked you to do it.
   7. The teacher ordered me to speak.
   8. My mother told me to do it again.

Reading and Conversation: The Liar

In the last lesson, we heard about Mark Twain and his friend on the train. He was so popular and famous in his day that there were many, many stories about him. Most of the stories were humorous. Here is another story to show his sense of humor.

One day Mark Twain was fishing. A stranger came along.

"Good morning!" said the stranger.

"Good morning!" said Twain. "This is good weather we're having."

"Very good weather," said the stranger. "Are you catching any fish?"

"The fishing is very good here. I caught three trout here yesterday in about an hour."

"Is that so?" said the stranger.

"Yes, and I'm very fond of trout."

"By the way," said the stranger, "do you happen to know who I am?"

"No, I haven't any idea," said Mark Twain.

"Well, I'm the game warden of this county," said the stranger, "and trout are out of season."

Mark Twain paused a minute. Then he asked, "By the way, do you know who I am?"

"No, I don't."

"Well, I'm the biggest liar in this county."

A. Comprehension and Conversation

1. What kinds of stories did people tell about Mark Twain in his day? Why did they tell the stories?
2. What was he doing when the stranger came along?
3. What did they say to each other?
4. Why did the stranger ask him if he caught any fish?
5. What did Mark Twain say in reply?
6. What kind of fish is trout? What kind of fish can you catch in the rivers near your home?
7. Who was the stranger? Why did this make Mark Twain nervous?
8. How did Mark Twain try to stay out of trouble with the man?
9. Do you enjoy fishing? Do you go fishing often?
10. What is a liar? Is it all right to lie sometimes?

B. Vocabulary

Nouns		*Verbs*	*Adjectives*
pear	syllable	guess	interesting
fish	capital	express	comparative
trout	game warden	disagree	superlative
county	command	believe	clever
weather	stranger	be fond of	humorous

C. Expressions

Use each of these expressions in a sentence.

sense of humor, Do you happen to know?, I have no idea, out of season, about an hour.

D. Pronunciation Drill

g as in <u>g</u>o, e<u>x</u>ample, e<u>gg</u>

good	forget	big
go	forgotten	dog
get	again	egg
girl	ago	leg

Phototeque

unit five

Dialogue

LUIS: Martha, I'm going to see the new Clint Eastwood movie tonight. Would you like to go with
me?

MARTHA: I have already seen that movie. I went last
night.

LUIS: Do you know if Janet has seen it, too?

MARTHA: Yes, she has seen it, too. We went together.
We've seen every movie Clint Eastwood has
ever made.

LUIS: Well, perhaps I'll change my mind. Let's go to
the Chinese restaurant for some dinner.

MARTHA: Good idea. I have eaten there before. It's an
excellent restaurant. They have good duck
dishes.

LUIS: They've been in business for a long time. My
aunt says that she remembers when it
opened. It's been there for at least twenty
years.

MARTHA: Have you ever had Thai food?

LUIS: Yes. I like it a lot.

MARTHA: Several friends have recommended the new
Thai restaurant to me. Perhaps we should go
there.

LUIS: Great. I haven't had Thai food in a long time.

Answer these questions:
1. Where does Luis want to go with Martha?
2. Why doesn't she want to go?
3. What did Janet do last night?
4. How do we know that Janet and Martha like Clint
Eastwood?
5. Do you like Clint Eastwood? Do you go to the movies often? How often?
6. Where do Luis and Martha decide to go to eat?
Why?
7. What did Luis's aunt say about the Chinese restaurant?

8. Does Luis speak English well? Why? Do you? Why/ Why not?
9. Do you like Chinese food? Do you go to Chinese restaurants often? When was the last time?
10. Do you like Thai food? What other types of food do you like?

Grammar and Usage

The Present Perfect Tense

a. To form the present perfect tense, we use *have (has)* plus the past participle of the verb.*

Singular	*Plural*
I have studied	we have studied
you have studied	you have studied
he she ⎬ has studied it	they have studied

The contracted form:

Singular	*Plural*
I've studied	we've studied
you've studied	you've studied
he's she's ⎬ studied it's	they've studied

b. The present perfect tense describes an action that is connected to the present but has occurred in the past.

I have read that book.
I have studied that lesson.
I have never been to Washington.

If the action took place at some definite time in the past, we use the simple past tense. Notice the difference in the following examples:

I *have studied* that lesson.
I *studied* that lesson *yesterday*.

---

* The past participle of regular verbs ends in -*ed* and is the same as the past tense. For the past participles of irregular verbs, see the Appendix.

c. We also use the present perfect tense to describe an action in the past which is repeated at indefinite periods.
   I have seen that movie *several times.*
   I have *often* visited them.

Exercises

A. Supply the present perfect tense of the verbs in parentheses.
   1. I have gone there many times. (go)
   2. She _____ in our house several times. (be)
   3. We _____ to them about it often. (speak)
   4. They _____ many stories about George Washington. (hear)
   5. He _____ me six letters. (write)
   6. It _____ every day this week. (rain)
   7. There _____ no snow since last winter. (be)
   8. Martha _____ in the restaurant several times. (eat)

B. Supply the correct tense, either the past or the present perfect.
   1. I wrote the letter yesterday. (write)
   2. He _____ to me several times, but he never remembers my name. (speak)
   3. I _____ him at the library in the literature room. (meet)
   4. I _____ that movie last night. (see)
   5. We _____ in that restaurant after the movie. (eat)
   6. We _____ Mexican food several times. (eat)
   7. He _____ to Europe by ship, but he returned by plane. (travel)
   8. She _____ to Chicago by train many times. (go)

C. Change these sentences from the past tense to the present perfect tense. Use contractions wherever possible. Add any words, such as *often, seldom, many times, several times,* necessary to complete the meaning of the new sentence.
   1. I saw her on the street last week. (I've often seen her on the street.)
   2. We were there last week.
   3. He stole a car.

4. It rained last night.
5. He flew to Caracas.
6. She asked the teacher for her grade.
7. I shook hands with the president.
8. They went to a farm.

Reading and Conversation:
George Washington and the Horse

George Washington was a well-known farmer and soldier before he became the first president of the United States. Here is one of the many anecdotes people told about him.

Once a neighbor stole one of Washington's horses. Washington went with a police officer to the neighbor's farm to get the horse, but the neighbor refused to give the horse up; he claimed that it was his horse.

Washington placed both of his hands over the eyes of the horse and said to the neighbor, "If this is your horse, then you must tell us in which eye he is blind."

"In the right eye!" the neighbor said.

Washington took his hand from the right eye of the horse and showed the police officer that the horse was not blind in the right eye.

"Oh, I have made a mistake," said the neighbor. "He is blind in the left eye."

Washington then showed that the horse was not blind in the left eye, either.

"I have made another mistake," said the neighbor.

"Yes," said the police officer, "and you have also shown us that you are a thief. This horse does not belong to you. You must return it to Mr. Washington."

A. Comprehension and Conversation

1. Who was George Washington?
2. What did his neighbor do?
3. Who went with George Washington to the neighbor's farm? Why?
4. How did George Washington prove that the horse did not belong to the neighbor?

5. Was the horse blind?
6. Do you know anyone who is blind? Any animals?
7. What do you think of this trick that Washington played on the neighbor?
8. What else do you know about George Washington?
9. What did the police officer do after Washington finished talking to the neighbor?
10. What is a thief? What are some other words which describe people who steal?

B. Vocabulary

Nouns		*Verbs*	*Adjectives*
aunt	library	open	Chinese
snow	soldier	claim	well known
farm	president	improve	blind
eye	anecdote	belong to	
thief	mistake	describe	*Adverbs*
horse	animal	shake hands	already
farmer	police officer	with	ever
		steal	
		refuse	

C. Expressions

Use each of these expressions in a sentence.
do you know, in business, at least, make a mistake.

D. Pronunciation Drill

b   as in bell, rubber, globe

be	about	job
big	rabbit	rib
bet	subscription	cab
bat	subtract	rob
barn	subject	robe
boot	able	rub

© Margot Granitsas

unit six

Dialogue

OLGA: Has Angela come home from work yet?

HARRY: No, she hasn't finished her work yet. She called to say that she had to stay longer than she planned.

OLGA: I haven't seen her since this morning. I was worried.

HARRY: Don't worry. She'll be O.K. Have you eaten dinner?

OLGA: No, I haven't had my dinner. I was waiting for you and Angela.

HARRY: How long have you waited?

OLGA: I've waited for about two hours. Where have you been?

HARRY: I've been at the library. I was studying for my exam in mathematics tomorrow. Up to now I haven't had any problems in that subject, but I want to get a good grade on the exam.

OLGA: How long have you studied math?

HARRY: For about two months. But, of course, people study math all their lives. Actually, I've studied math since I was a child.

OLGA: Has Angela taken that course, too?

HARRY: I don't think she has taken any course in math since she was in elementary school. Let's not wait anymore. Let's have dinner.

OLGA: O.K.

Answer these questions:
1. Why isn't Angela home from work yet?
2. Has Olga eaten dinner? Why?
3. How long has she waited for Harry and Angela?
4. Where has Harry been? Why?
5. How long has he studied math?
6. Has Angela taken any math courses lately?
7. Have you ever been late for dinner? Why?
8. Has anyone in your home ever waited for you or worried about you? What happened?
9. Have you taken any math classes lately? When?
10. Have you visited the library lately? Have you studied for any examinations lately?

Grammar and Usage

1. The Present Perfect Tense: Negative and Question Forms

a. The present perfect tense describes an action which began in the past and continues into the present.

He *lived* here for two years. (in 1982 and 1983)
He *has lived* here for two years. (He is still living here.)

b. We form the negative of the present perfect tense by placing *not* after *have (has)*.

Singular	*Plural*
I have *not* studied	we have *not* studied
you have *not* studied	you have *not* studied
he	
she } has *not* studied	they have *not* studied
it	

The contracted form:

Singular	*Plural*
I haven't studied	we haven't studied
you haven't studied	you haven't studied
he	
she } hasn't studied	they haven't studied
it	

c. We form the question of the present perfect tense by placing *have (has)* in front of the subject.

He has worked here for two years.
Has he worked here for two years?
How long has he worked here?
They have gone home.
Have they gone home?
Where have they gone?

2. *For* and *since*

a. *For* shows general duration of time in the past, present, or future.

I have gone there every summer *for* a week's vacation.
I went there every summer *for* a week's vacation.

I go there every summer *for* a week's vacation.
I will go there every summer *for* a week's vacation.

b. *Since* shows duration of time from the past to the present. We always use *since* with the present perfect tense.
I have gone there every summer *since* 1980.
He has worked there *since* last year.

Exercises

A. Underline the correct form.
   1. She has lived in that house (since, for) three years.
   2. He (moved, has moved) to California in 1981.
   3. Jacob (studied, has studied) English for four years.
   4. (Has, Did) she attend the university last year?
   5. (Has, Did) Mr. Nava always lived with you?
   6. My present teacher is Ms. Sasaki. I (was, have been) in her class for two months.
   7. They have been married (since, for) 1979.
   8. She has worn her hair short (since, for) about a year.

B. Change these sentences to the negative form. Use contractions.
   1. He has heard that anecdote before. (He hasn't heard that anecdote before.)
   2. It's rained for two days now.
   3. We've made a lot of mistakes.
   4. I've answered your letter.
   5. They've depended on their parents for help for years.
   6. You've always sat in the first row.
   7. Roberto and Harry have seen that movie.
   8. You and I have been to New York.

C. Repeat Exercise B, changing the sentences to questions.
   1. He has heard that anecdote before. (Has he heard that anecdote before?)

D. Fill in the blanks with the past participle form of each of these verbs.

see	_____	hide	_____
leave	_____	go	_____
shake	_____	prove	_____
fly	_____	enjoy	_____
be	_____	smile	_____

do	————————	depend	————————
make	————————	wear	————————
speak	————————	come	————————

E. Change the following present tense sentences first to the past tense, then to the present perfect tense. Add or subtract any words necessary to complete the meanings.
  1. He sits near me. (He sat near me yesterday. He has sat near me all year.)
  2. She goes to the movies every week.
  3. Does he make much money at his job?
  4. We always smile at her.
  5. The leaves fall from the tree.
  6. It rains in the spring.
  7. There are two students in that room.
  8. Do you drive to work every day?

Reading and Conversation: A Joke on a Humorist

Mark Twain was famous as a writer, as we have seen, but he was also famous as a public speaker and teller of funny stories. He often went from town to town giving lectures.

One day he was walking along the street of a small town where he was going to deliver a lecture that evening. He met a young man who said, "Mr. Twain, I'd like to talk to you for a minute, please. I have an uncle that I'm very fond of. The problem is he never laughs or smiles. Can you do anything?"

"Bring your uncle to my lecture this evening, young man. I guarantee that he'll laugh and smile. Don't worry about a thing."

That evening the young man and his uncle sat in the first row. Mark Twain spoke directly at them. He told some very funny stories, but the old man never smiled. Then he told the funniest stories he knew, but the old man's face still remained blank. At last, Mark Twain left the platform almost exhausted.

Later Mark Twain was talking with a friend about this.

"Oh!" said the friend. "I know that old man. He has been stone deaf for years."

A. Comprehension and Conversation

1. What was Mark Twain famous for? What else was Twain famous for?
2. Why was he walking down the street?
3. Who approached him? What did he say?
4. What did Twain suggest?
5. How do you think Twain felt when the old man didn't laugh at his stories? How would you have felt?
6. What did he later discover about the old man?
7. Do you know anyone who is deaf? How do deaf people communicate?
8. Do you enjoy lectures? What was the last lecture you attended?
9. Have you ever given a lecture? Would you like to give one? On what topic?
10. Do you know any funny stories? Tell one.

B. Vocabulary

Nouns	Verbs		Adjectives
course	attend	fall	deaf
row	smile	deliver	blank
teller	approach	wait for	exhausted
topic	suggest	depend on	
university	be worried		Adverbs
child	be married		actually
lecture	guarantee		lately

C. Expressions

Use each of these expressions in a sentence.
up to now, of course, from town to town, stone deaf.

D. Pronunciation Drill

Point out the silent letters (letters which are not pronounced) in each of the following words; then practice the words.

listen	sign	neighbor	friend
talk	walk	write	design
Wednesday	know	answer	autumn
deaf	heard	building	rhyme

San Antonio Convention and Visitors Bureau

unit seven

Dialogue

TONY: Where were you last week, Julia? I called you on Monday, Wednesday, and Friday.

JULIA: By Monday I had already left on my vacation.

TONY: Where did you go?

JULIA: I visited many of the places in Texas that I knew as a little girl.

TONY: I'll bet that was fun! Did you meet any old friends?

JULIA: Yes, I saw a lot of people I went to school with. They had changed so much that I didn't recognize some of them. But then they mentioned some of the things we had done as children, some of the parties we had attended, some of the times we had had together. Then I remembered.

TONY: Did you visit your cousin Carmen?

JULIA: I wanted to visit her, but when I arrived, she had already left. She now lives in Canada.

TONY: Hadn't your brother just visited you here?

JULIA: Yes, but I hadn't seen the other members of my family for years.

TONY: Well, I'm glad you're back.

Answer these questions:
1. What had Julia already done when Tony called her on Monday?
2. Where did she go?
3. What did she do there?
4. Why didn't she recognize some of her old friends at first? How did she finally recognize them?
5. Did she visit her cousin? Why/Why not?
6. Had her brother just visited her? Had she seen the other members of her family recently?
7. Had you already taken an English class before you started this one? What was it called?

8. How long had you studied English before this class began?
9. Had you met the other students in this class before the course began? How?
10. Do you remember doing things when you were a very young child? What things?

Grammar and Usage

The Past Perfect Tense

a. To form the past perfect tense, we use *had* plus the past participle of the verb.

Singular	*Plural*
I had gone	we had gone
you had gone	you had gone
he she it } had gone	they had gone

The contracted form:

Singular	*Plural*
I'd gone	we'd gone
you'd gone	you'd gone
he'd she'd } gone	they'd gone

b. We form the negative of the past perfect tense by placing *not* after *had*.

Singular	*Plural*
I had *not* gone	we had *not* gone
you had *not* gone	you had *not* gone
he she it } had *not* gone	they had *not* gone

The contracted form:

Singular	*Plural*
I hadn't gone	we hadn't gone
you hadn't gone	you hadn't gone
he she it } hadn't gone	they hadn't gone

    c. We form the question of the past perfect tense by placing *had* in front of the subject.

          He had lived there a year when she met him.

          Had he lived there a year when she met him?

          How long *had* he lived there when she met him?

    d. We use the past perfect tense to describe an action which took place before some definite point in past time. Therefore, we do not use the past perfect tense alone, but always in connection with some stated or implied past tense.

          He *had left* when we arrived.

          He said he *had seen* that movie.

Exercises

    A. Supply the past perfect tense of the verbs in parentheses.

      1. The doctor had gone when we got there. (go)

      2. They _____ already _____ when I called. (eat)

      3. He _____ the egg when she arrived. (boil)

      4. He discovered that the old man _____ every one of his lectures. (attend)

      5. She said she _____ already _____ the book. (read)

      6. I told him that I _____ the medicine. (take)

      7. We _____ an hour for the bus before we found out that it wasn't coming. (wait)

      8. She said that she _____ that movie before. (see)

    B. Change the tense in these sentences from past to past perfect. Begin each sentence with *he said that* or *she told me that*.

      1. They saw the movie. (She told me that they had seen the movie.)

      2. He took the medicine.

      3. She went to the doctor.

      4. He enjoyed the lecture.

      5. Someone stole the book.

      6. You played in Friday's football game.

      7. She returned immediately after receiving the message.

      8. I entered the wrong room.

C. Change these sentences to the negative form. Use contractions.
   1. He had left when we arrived. (He hadn't left when we arrived.)
   2. They had eaten their dinner by seven o'clock.
   3. She had taken her medicine when I saw her.
   4. We had already seen the movie.
   5. She had gone when I called.
   6. You had had your lunch.
   7. They had heard the joke.
   8. It had rained for a week.

D. Repeat Exercise C, changing the sentences to questions.
   1. He had left when we arrived. (Had he left when we arrived?)

Reading and Conversation:
Isaac Newton and the Egg

There are many stories about absent-minded people. For example, a professor was once walking down the street when one of his students happened to pass him. "Which way am I walking, north or south?" asked the professor.

"North," said the student.

"Good!" said the professor. "Then I have had my lunch."

There is another story of a similar kind about Isaac Newton, the famous scientist. Newton was also a very absent-minded man. Once his assistant came into his laboratory with an egg which she wanted to cook. She wanted to boil it over his alcohol lamp. Newton was busy thinking about some problem and wished to be alone. He asked her to leave. He said that he would boil her egg for her. The assistant gave Newton her watch and told him to boil the egg for exactly three minutes.

A little while later, the assistant returned. Newton was still thinking about his problem with the egg in his hand. The watch, however, was boiling merrily in the water.

A. Comprehension and Conversation

1. What do we mean when we say that a person is absent-minded?

2. Do you know any absent-minded people? Are you absent-minded? Give some examples.
3. In the first part of the story, why did the professor ask the student which way he was walking?
4. In the second part of the story, who came into Newton's laboratory?
5. What did Newton ask her to do? Why?
6. What did she give him? Why?
7. What mistake did Newton make with the egg and the watch?
8. Do you eat eggs? How do you like to cook them?
9. What is an assistant? What jobs would an assistant do in a laboratory?
10. Why is Isaac Newton famous?

B. Vocabulary

Nouns	*Verbs*	*Adjectives*
children	bet	absent-minded
football	be glad	north
medicine	mention	south
assistant	recognize	similar
alcohol lamp	attend	
parties	plan	*Adverbs*
doctor	boil	still
scientist		merrily
laboratory		

C. Expressions

Use each of these expressions in a sentence.
I'll bet, gone to school with, old friends, back home, a little while later.

D. Pronunciation Drill

ʃ   as in <u>sh</u>oe, ac<u>ti</u>on, fi<u>sh</u>

shop	fashion	wish	mention
share	ocean	wash	bushel
she	election	push	depression
shall	delicious	rush	exception

© *Margot Granitsas*

unit eight

Dialogue

CLERK: Good evening.

JULIO: Good evening. My wife and I would like a room, please. Do you have one? We don't have a reservation.

CLERK: Yes, we have a lot of rooms available. This is not our busy season. I can give you a quiet room away from the highway. It has two double beds.

JULIO: How much is it for one night? We only need it for tonight. We're going to continue our trip in the morning.

CLERK: It's forty dollars a night for two people.

JULIO: Is there air conditioning? I hope so. It's so hot today.

CLERK: Yes. The switch is on the right as you enter the room. Please turn the air conditioner off when you leave the room.

JULIO: Is there a store where I can buy an umbrella? I think it's going to rain.

CLERK: No, the only store nearby is an antique shop. If you're hungry, our restaurant is open until eleven o'clock.

JULIO: Thank you. May I pay for this with a credit card, or do you want cash?

CLERK: A credit card will be O.K. Here's your key to room 25. I hope you enjoy your stay with us.

Answer these questions:
1. Where does this dialogue take place? Between what two people?
2. What is a *reservation?* How does a person usually make a reservation?
3. What is the difference between a hotel and a motel?
4. How much did the room cost for two people for one night?
5. How much does a motel room in your town cost for two people for one night?
6. What is *air conditioning?* Why do you think the clerk asked Julio to turn off the air conditioner when he left the room?

7. Why did Julio ask the clerk where he could buy an umbrella?
8. What is an *antique shop?* Have you ever been to an antique shop? What did you see?
9. Do you have a credit card? (Or does someone in your family have one?) What do you use it for?
10. What are the names of some hotels and motels in your area?

Grammar and Usage

Articles

a. We use the definite article *the* before both singular and plural nouns of definite or particular meaning.
   The book is on *the* table.
   The books are on *the* tables.

b. We use the indefinite articles *a* and *an* before singular nouns of indefinite or general meaning. We use *a* before nouns beginning with a consonant sound; we use *an* before nouns beginning with a vowel sound.
   Do you have *a* reservation?
   He wants to buy *an* umbrella.
   They don't live in *a* hotel.
   I'll be there in *an* hour.

c. We do not use articles before mass nouns, that is, things that cannot be counted. However, if these nouns represent a particular sample of the thing, we use the definite article.
   Water is necessary for everyone.
   The water in this glass is not clear.
   Gold is an important metal.
   The gold in this ring is very beautiful.

d. We do not use articles before the names of cities, streets, countries, or persons unless they are used as adjectives.
   San Francisco is a beautiful city.
   The San Francisco earthquake was in 1906.
   I live on Sixth Street.
   The Sixth Street stores stay open until nine in the evening.

e. We do not use articles when a noun is modified by a person's name or by a possessive pronoun.
   Nancy's house is next to my house.

f. Indefinite articles may be used idiomatically in expressions of time, distance, and quantity.

That train can travel at sixty miles per hour.
That train can travel at sixty miles *an* hour.
In that store, eggs cost $1.25 for twelve.
In that store, eggs cost $1.25 *a* dozen.

Exercises

A. One sentence in each of the following pairs requires an article; the other does not. Fill in articles only where needed.
1. _____ good food is necessary for good health.
2. _____ food in that restaurant is good.
3. I studied _____ history of the United States last year.
4. I like to study _____ history.
5. Sometimes sick people have to take _____ medicine.
6. _____ medicine which the doctor gave me helped my cough.
7. Some people say that they do not need _____ money.
8. I found _____ money that you lost.
9. _____ New York buses are modern and comfortable.
10. _____ New York is a large city.
11. We took a walk along _____ Pennsylvania Avenue.
12. There was a meeting of _____ Pennsylvania Avenue merchants last night.
13. They have an office in New York, but send it to _____ France address.
14. Someday I want to visit _____ France.
15. My favorite department store is _____ I. Magnin.
16. _____ I. Magnin sale is almost over.

B. Some of the following sentences require articles; others do not. Fill in articles only where needed.
1. There is _____ pencil on the desk.
2. I think I've lost _____ pencil that you gave me.
3. She always drinks _____ coffee with her breakfast.
4. What time do you usually have _____ lunch?

5. He placed _____ large stone in the middle of the road.
6. English is not _____ difficult language to learn.
7. Would you like to have _____ cup of coffee with me?
8. My family bought _____ new car last week.

C. Use the indefinite article idiomatically.
1. They cost me $20 for each pair. (They cost me $20 a pair.)
2. They cost me $50 for each dozen.
3. The plane travels at 550 miles per hour.
4. The motel room was $40 for each night.
5. The gloves were $15 for each pair.
6. He studies four hours each day.
7. My rent is $400 for each month.
8. Our class meets five times each week.

Reading and Conversation: Visitors in Miami

A couple from another country was once visiting Miami. They wanted to take a walk and to see the city, but they were afraid they might get lost. They did not speak any English.

After they left their hotel, they went to the first street corner and looked at the names of the two streets. Then they carefully copied the two names into their notebook. They thought that this would help them find their way back if they got lost.

They walked for hours through the city, and suddenly they realized that they were lost. They found a police officer and asked for help, but the officer didn't speak their native language.

After an hour they found a person who could help them. She was an interpreter who spoke both their native language and English. They explained that they didn't know the name of their hotel, but they knew which corner it was on. They showed the interpreter what they had copied into their notebook, and the interpreter began to laugh.

The words which they had so carefully copied were *Stop* and *One Way*.

A. Comprehension and Conversation

1. Where was the couple in the story from? Where were they visiting?
2. What did they want to do? What was their fear?
3. What did they write in their notebook? Why?
4. What happened when they took their walk?
5. Why did they ask the police officer for help?
6. What is an *interpreter?* What can one do?
7. What did the interpreter in the story try to do for the couple from another country?
8. Why did the interpreter laugh when she read their notebook?
9. What does *stop* mean? What is a one-way street?
10. What would you do if you got lost in a strange city?

B. Vocabulary

Nouns

reservation	switch	sale	interpreter
double bed	cash	gold	department store
air conditioning	stay	fire	meeting
antique shop	hotel	fear	merchants
credit card	motel	metal	

Verbs	*Adjectives*		*Other*
get lost	busy	available	nearby
copy	quiet	hungry	next to
take a walk	afraid	important	

C. Expressions

Use each of these expressions in a sentence.
I hope so, on the right, stay open until . . . , . . . miles an hour.

D. Pronunciation Drill

r as in right, hurry, store

room	proud	very	car
run	try	direction	purr
red	tree	marry	her
ride	drive	story	fear

Pierre Cardin/Palma Kolansky

unit nine

Dialogue

SALLY: I like that raincoat you're wearing, Laura. Is it yours?

LAURA: No, it's not mine. I forgot my raincoat today, so I borrowed this from Gina. It's hers. This umbrella that I'm carrying is hers, too.

SALLY: It seems that you forgot several things today. Do you remember if this is our classroom?

LAURA: Yes, it's ours. I wouldn't forget this room. Pedro and Barry always leave their books on the table in the back of the room. See? There they are. Those are Pedro's and Barry's books.

SALLY: Are you sure those books are theirs? I thought they were the teacher's books.

LAURA: I'm sure. Let's look inside to be certain.

SALLY: Yes, this is Pedro's book. His name is inside the front cover. I'll bet this notebook is his, too. *(She looks inside the notebook.)* Yes, this is his.

LAURA: Sally, I have a problem. I also forgot a pencil today. May I borrow yours?

SALLY: You should try to remember such important items. If you have a bad memory, you ought to write yourself a note. Here. You may use this pen, but please remember when class is over that it's mine.

LAURA: I will, and thank you.

Answer these questions:
1. What does Sally wonder about Laura's raincoat?
2. Whose raincoat is it?
3. What else did Laura borrow? From whom? Why?
4. How does Laura know that they are in the right classroom?
5. How are the girls certain that the book belongs to Pedro?
6. What is Laura's other problem today? How does she solve it?

7. Do you have a good memory? How do you help your-self remember things?
8. What should a person with a bad memory do?
9. What items do you sometimes borrow from friends? Do you always remember to return them?
10. Is the book that you have in your hand yours? Is the book in your teacher's hand his/hers?

Grammar and Usage

1. Possessive Pronouns

The possessive adjectives *(my, your, his, her, our, their)* when used alone as pronouns have the following forms.

my – mine	our – ours
your – yours	your – yours
his – his	their – theirs
her – hers	

This pencil is my pencil.
   This pencil is *mine.*
That eraser is our eraser.
   That eraser is *ours.*

2. *Should/ought*

Should and *ought* are auxiliary verbs which are used to express obligation. They have more or less the same mean-ing and can be used interchangeably. They are weaker in force than *must* and sometimes have even a negative sig-nificance. Note that *ought* is followed by the infinitive with *to.*

I *should* study tonight (but it is possible that I will not study).
I *ought* to study tonight.
He *should* not smoke so much. He *should*n't smoke so much.
He *ought* not to smoke so much.

Exercises

A. Substitute possessive pronouns for the italicized words.
1. That is *her pen*. (That is hers.)
2. Those are *his books*.
3. That is *my history book*.
4. That is *her coat*.
5. These are *the students' desks*.
6. Those are *your pencils*.
7. These are *our scarves*.
8. This is *my aunt's air conditioner*.

B. Rewrite these sentences introducing a possessive pronoun.
1. The key belongs to her. (The key is hers.)
2. The pears belong to you.
3. The trout belongs to me.
4. The horse doesn't belong to them.
5. The farm doesn't belong to us.
6. Does this sandwich belong to her?
7. Do those bags belong to him?
8. Doesn't this shampoo belong to me?

C. Rewrite these sentences using the verb *belong to* instead of *be*.
1. These flowers are mine. (These flowers belong to me.)
2. Is this homework yours?
3. That picture is hers.
4. Is this bottle of ammonia his?
5. These books are not ours.
6. Those fish are theirs.
7. Are these messages yours?
8. That medicine isn't mine.

D. Fill in the blanks first with *should* + the verb in parentheses, then with *ought to* + the verb in parentheses.
1. Helen _____ more. (study) (Helen should study more. Helen ought to study more.)
2. I _____ more time on my English lessons. (spend)
3. He _____ his medicine every day. (take)
4. You _____ a reservation first. (make)
5. We _____ not _____ late at night. (stay out)

6. People _____ not _____ so much. (smoke)
7. Your sister _____ tonight. (study)
8. Your friend _____ when he meets people for the first time. (shake hands)

Reading and Conversation:
George Washington and the Corporal

During the revolutionary war, General George Washington was riding through the country in civilian clothes. He came upon four soldiers who were trying to remove a tree which had fallen across the road. Only three of the men were working. The fourth stood alongside. He was directing the others and cursing at them because they were unable to remove the tree. Washington stopped and asked why he was not helping the others.

"I am an officer," the man said. "I am a corporal in the Continental army."

Washington got down off his horse, took off his coat, and helped the three men. Soon they removed the tree. After this the corporal asked Washington what his name was.

"I am also an officer," Washington said. "My name is George Washington, commander in chief of the Continental army."

A. Comprehension and Conversation

1. Where was Washington riding? What was he wearing?
2. What is the difference between civilian clothes and military clothes?
3. Why were the three soldiers working?
4. What was the fourth soldier doing while the others were working?
5. What was his explanation to Washington?
6. What did Washington then do?
7. How do you think the corporal felt when he found out who Washington was? How would you have felt?
8. If you were in the army, would you rather be a corporal or a general? Why?

9. What is the job of an officer?
10. What does *cursing* mean? Why do people sometimes curse?

B. Vocabulary

Nouns	*Verbs*	*Adjectives*	*Adverbs*
raincoat	wonder	sure	inside
thing	get down	military	alongside
item	come upon	civilian	
soldier	curse	certain	
corporal	forget	front	
explanation	take off		
general			
umbrella			
cover			
memory			
officer			
army			
purpose			

C. Expressions

Use each of these expressions in a sentence.
revolutionary war, Are you sure? inside the front cover.

D. Pronunciation Drill

Note that when we add the past or past participle ending *-ed* to a regular verb which ends in *-d* or *-t,* we pronounce the *-ed* as a separate syllable; when the verb ends in any other letter, we do not pronounce the *-ed* as a separate syllable. Therefore, the verbs in the first two columns below are pronounced as words of two syllables; the verbs in the last two columns are pronounced as words of one syllable only.

wanted	ended	liked	lived
counted	needed	walked	used
handed	lasted	asked	stopped
waited	shouted	learned	placed

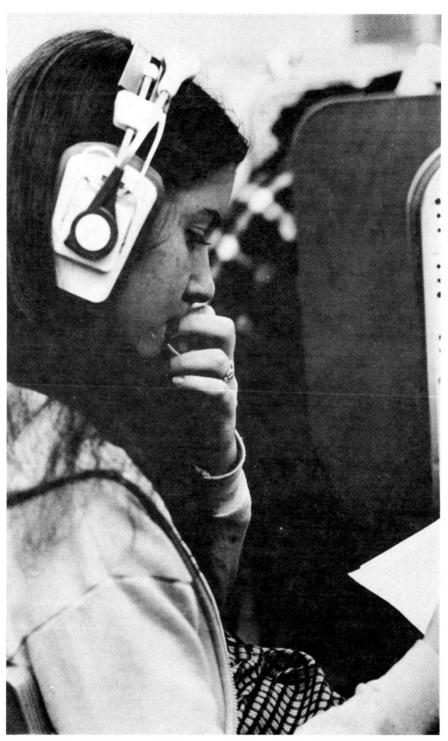

© Laimute E. Druskis

unit ten

Vocabulary

A. Fill in the blanks with the opposites of the following words:

down	_____ up _____	stop	_____
north	_____	forget	_____
inside	_____	sad	_____
left	_____	civilian	_____
pull	_____	little	_____
best	_____	weak	_____
quiet	_____	take off	_____
front	_____	clever	_____
open	_____	children	_____
boyfriend	_____	poor	_____

B. Supply the correct preposition:
1. He is leaving for New York in the morning.
2. She came here _____ plane.
3. He placed his hands _____ the eyes _____ the horse.
4. The horse was not blind _____ the right eye.
5. It does not belong _____ me.
6. That restaurant serves lunch _____ one o'clock.
7. They complained _____ the food.
8. You can always depend _____ him.
9. I asked the doctor to give me something _____ my cough.
10. She is _____ England. She was born _____ London.

C. Fill in the blanks with the correct past and past participle forms of the following verbs:

be fond of	was fond of	been fond of
steal	_____	_____
attend	_____	_____
fall	_____	_____
wait for	_____	_____
bet	_____	_____
boil	_____	_____

shake hands with	_____	_____
choose	_____	_____
hide	_____	_____
put on	_____	_____
push	_____	_____
get along	_____	_____
lie	_____	_____
sit	_____	_____
copy	_____	_____
take a walk	_____	_____
curse	_____	_____
come upon	_____	_____
forget	_____	_____

D. Underline the correct answer.
   1. A person who knows two languages may work as (a doctor, a general, a lecturer, an interpreter).
   2. A person who cannot see is (deaf, blind, exhausted, blank).
   3. If you feel hot, what will you probably do with your coat? (put it on, take it off, pick it up, come upon it)
   4. Which of these words is not spelled correctly? (anecdote, guarante, corporal, usually)
   5. Which of these words is a past participle? (took, saw, came, done)
   6. Which of these words rhymes with *great?* (hat, get, plate, treat)
   7. We pronounce the contraction *she's* to rhyme with (piece, please, his, miss).
   8. In which of these can you travel fastest? (train, car, bus, plane)
   9. Which of these is a two-syllable word? (wanted, walked, hoped, rained)
   10. Which of the following people is in the army? (police officer, president, farmer, corporal)

Grammar

A. Change these sentences to the present perfect tense. Add any words necessary to complete the meaning. Use contractions.
   1. I wrote him a letter. (I've written him a letter.)
   2. She answered the phone.

    3. You never visit me.
    4. They lived in New York for three years.
    5. We never went to Florence.
    6. Mary didn't make a mistake.
    7. The old man didn't smile.
    8. Did he study English at that school?
    9. Did you bring me my books?
   10. Did I meet you?

B. Change these sentences to simple questions.
    1. John saw that movie. (Did John see that movie?)
    2. It rains in Arizona in August.
    3. They want to go to Jamaica on their vacation.
    4. We will be in Philadelphia next week.
    5. She is going to fly to Spain in December.
    6. You were sleeping in class.
    7. Tom is staying home today.
    8. You have lived here for several years.
    9. He had left before she arrived.
   10. It hasn't snowed yet this winter.

C. Underline the correct form.
    1. I didn't see (someone, <u>anyone</u>) in the room.
    2. She is the (<u>most beautiful</u>, beautifulest) horse on the farm.
    3. I (saw, have seen) the movie yesterday.
    4. You ought (study, to study) more.
    5. That book is yours, but this one is (my, mine).
    6. She has studied English (since, for) three years.
    7. They wanted (that we wait, us to wait) for them after class.
    8. (Who, Whom) did you speak to?
    9. Tomorrow night we are going to stay at (a, an) hotel.
   10. He doesn't have (any, some) friends in Texas.

Puerto Rico Tourism Development Company

unit eleven

Dialogue

MS. NASH: Diego, when were you born?

DIEGO: I was born January 28, 1974. I was born in Bolivia.

MS. NASH: Good. Gina, do you know whom this book was written by?

GINA: Yes, it was written by Robert Dixson.

MS. NASH: And do you know whom this class is usually taught by?

GINA: This class is usually taught by you, Ms. Nash. However, last week this class wasn't taught by you. You were on vacation. Last week it was taught by Mr. Tanaka.

MS. NASH: Dolores, is it true that your sister got married yesterday? I heard that she went to San Juan.

DOLORES: Yes, it's true. She was married in San Juan, Puerto Rico. They were married yesterday morning.

MS. NASH: Andrew, who usually cooks the meals in your family?

ANDREW: The meals are usually cooked by my mother, but last week some were cooked by my father, and next week some will be cooked by my brother and me. We're all going camping.

MS. NASH: Good. Thank you, Andrew. Don't forget the English test. It'll be given next Wednesday. I hope you'll study hard for it.

Answer these questions:
1. When were you born? Where were you born?
2. Whom was this book written by?
3. Is your English class usually taught by a man or a woman?
4. What happened to Dolores's sister?
5. What did Andrew say about meals in his house?
6. Are the meals in your house always cooked by the same person? Are they ever cooked by you?
7. When will your next English test be given?

8. When was America discovered? By whom?
9. When was the Declaration of Independence signed? Where?
10. When were your parents married? Where?

Grammar and Usage

The Passive Voice

a. We form the passive voice by using the verb *to be* as an auxiliary, plus the past participle of the main verb. For every active voice tense, there is a corresponding passive form.

	Active Voice	*Passive Voice*
Present	She brings the mail.	The mail is brought.
Past	She brought the mail.	The mail was brought.
Future	She will bring the mail.	The mail will be brought.
Present Perfect	She has brought the mail.	The mail has been brought.
Past Perfect	She had brought the mail.	The mail had been brought.

b. When the subject of the sentence acts, we use the active voice.
    She brings the mail.

When the subject receives the action, we use the passive voice.
    The mail is brought (by her).

c. When the agent who performs the action is unknown or unimportant, we use the passive voice.
    English *is spoken* in many countries.
    That building *was built* in 1972.
    They *will be married* in a church.
    The package *has* already *been delivered*.

d. We form the passive voice negative by placing *not* after the auxiliary. We form passive voice questions by placing the auxiliary before the subject.
    The money was *not* stolen by him. (The money wasn't stolen by him.)
    Was the money stolen by him?

Exercises

A. Change these sentences to the passive voice.
1. We cut the grass yesterday. (The grass was cut by us yesterday.)
2. We usually cut the grass once a week.
3. We will cut the grass tomorrow.
4. I have put the food on the table.
5. She wrote it many years ago.
6. The cat ate the food quickly.
7. They had removed the tree from the road.
8. I'll clean the floor tomorrow.

B. Change these sentences to the active voice.
1. The newspaper was bought by my uncle. (My uncle bought the newspaper.)
2. The book was written by Thomas Mann.
3. The work will be done by her aunt.
4. That magazine is read by me every month.
5. The dishes are washed by them after every meal.
6. The keys have been found by the soldier.
7. The snake had been stolen by the zoo employee.
8. He has been taken to the university by his brother.

C. Change these sentences to the negative form. Use contractions.
1. The letter was signed by the president. (The letter wasn't signed by the president.)
2. He had been taken to a police station.
3. She has been seen at the library.
4. The lecture was delivered by the game warden.
5. The book was written by a friend of Mr. Hall.
6. The tickets will be bought by a young boy.
7. The letters have been signed.
8. Mathematics is studied in that school.

D. Repeat Exercise C changing the sentences first to simple questions, then to questions beginning with words like *how, by whom, why, where,* or *what.*
1. The letter was signed by the president. (Was the letter signed by the president? What was signed by the president? By whom was the letter signed?)

Reading and Conversation:
Two Mark Twain Stories

As we have already seen, Mark Twain was a very clever man. He could think quickly, and he had a good sense of humor. We don't know if these two stories are true, but they are interesting anyway.

Mark Twain went to a certain friend to ask him a favor.

"I'd like to borrow a book from your library."

"I'm sorry," replied the friend. "I never permit books to be taken from my library. If you want to read the book, you must read it here in the library. You may not take it home."

A few days later, this same friend wanted to mow his lawn. So he went to Mark Twain's house to borrow his lawn mower.

"I'm sorry," said Twain. "I never permit my lawn mower to be taken from my home. If you want to use it, you must use it here."

Another time, Twain's nephew was visiting him. One morning, when they both went down to breakfast, Twain saw that his nephew's shoes were dirty.

"Your shoes are covered with mud. Why didn't you clean them last night? he asked the boy.

"I thought it was useless to clean them in such bad weather," the nephew replied. "They will only get dirty again in a short time." Twain then prepared his breakfast, but he made nothing for the boy.

"Why is there no breakfast for me?" the nephew asked.

"I thought it was useless for you to eat," said Twain, "because you will only get hungry again in a short time."

A. Comprehension and Conversation

1. Do you think these stories about Mark Twain are true? Why/Why not?
2. What did Mark Twain want to borrow from his friend?
3. What did the friend tell him?
4. What did the friend later want to borrow from Mark Twain?
5. What do you think of the reply Twain made to the friend?

6. In the second story, why didn't Mark Twain's nephew want to clean his shoes?
7. Why didn't Twain prepare any breakfast for his nephew?
8. What lessons can be learned from these two stories?
9. Do you clean your shoes when they are covered with mud? Why/Why not?
10. What is a *lawn mower?* Have you ever used a lawn mower? How do they work?

B. Vocabulary

Nouns	Verbs		Adjectives
lawn mower	be born	get married	true
magazine	cook	teach	useless
nephew	cut	happen to	dirty
meal	clean	reply	
grass	permit	prepare	
mud	be covered		*Adverbs*
cat	with		quickly
			anyway

C. Expressions

Use each of these expressions in a sentence.
the Declaration of Independence, in order to, last night, a short time.

D. Pronunciation Drill

The ending *-ed,* when added to any regular verb to form the simple past tense or the past participle, is pronounced as follows:
1. as a separate syllable if the verb ends in *t* or *d.*
   wait – waited   add – added
2. as *t* if the verb ends in a voiceless sound (except *t*).
   ask – asked   wash – washed
3. As *d* if the verb ends in a voiced sound (except *d*).
   play – played   turn – turned

Practice these past tense sounds:

walked	learned	needed	used
counted	lived	expected	answered
liked	waited	attended	finished
watched	wanted	listened	ended

Winnebago Industries, Inc.

unit twelve

Dialogue

CATHY: What are you doing with that knife, Andrew? Be careful that you don't cut yourself.

ANDREW: It's too late. I have already cut myself trying to cut this meat.

CATHY: Do you want me to help you?

ANDREW: No, I can do it by myself.

KEVIN: Cathy, what is Andrew doing?

CATHY: He's cutting the meat.

KEVIN: By himself? Doesn't he want help?

CATHY: No, he said he wanted to do it himself. Children his age *like* to do things for themselves.

KEVIN: What happened to your hand?

CATHY: I burned myself trying to light the fire.

KEVIN: You shouldn't try to light the fire by yourself. I hope Andrew doesn't cut himself with that knife.

CATHY: He already *has* cut himself.

KEVIN: Ow! *(holding his foot)* Who left the tent supplies in the path? Now we've all hurt ourselves. What a family!

Answer these questions:
1. What is the difference between "He hurt *him*" and "He hurt *himself*"?
2. Do cats always wash themselves, or do people have to wash them? Do you have a cat?
3. Have you ever cut yourself with a knife? How did it happen?
4. Have you ever burned yourself? Has anyone in your family ever burned himself or herself? How?
5. Do you live by yourself or with your family? Do you know anyone who lives by himself or herself?
6. Do you like to go to the movies by yourself or with friends? Have you ever gone to the movies by yourself?

7. What did Kevin say to Cathy about lighting the fire?
8. When you have to cut something, do you like to do it yourself, or do you ask someone for help?
9. Can you do all the exercises in this book yourself?
10. How are the three people in the dialogue related?

Grammar and Usage

1. Reflexive Pronouns

a. The reflexive pronouns are the following:

I – myself	we – ourselves
you – yourself	you – yourselves
he – himself	
she – herself	they – themselves
it – itself	

b. We use reflexive pronouns to refer back to the subject of the sentence. The subject and the object are the same.
    He hurt himself.
    We burned ourselves.

c. We also use reflexive pronouns emphatically, that is, to give emphasis to some person or thing in the sentence.
    They themselves will do it.
    She can do it herself.

d. We use reflexive pronouns with *by* to mean "alone" or "without help."
    I went to the city *by myself.*
    Do you like to go to the movies *by yourself?*

2. *Who/whose*

The possessive case form of *who* is *whose. Whose* may be used both as a question pronoun and as a relative pronoun.
    Whose book is this?
    The man *whose* son you met is waiting outside.

Exercises

A. Supply the correct reflexive pronoun.
1. Cathy burned <u>herself</u> badly.

2. Her brother also burned _____.
3. Have you ever burned _____ badly?
4. Can you hear _____ when you talk?
5. We didn't enjoy _____ at the movie.
6. I cut _____ with that knife.
7. Mary said that she enjoyed _____ at the theater.
8. Did both of the boys cut _____ with that knife?

B. Supply the correct reflexive pronoun for emphatic purposes.
1. Mary said that she <u>herself</u> saw him do it.
2. They _____ carried the boxes.
3. He _____ will cut the grass.
4. We _____ saw him take the money.
5. I _____ went to the farm.
6. We _____ will have to prove the answer correct.
7. Have you _____ seen it happen?
8. Did she _____ go to the theater?

C. Delete the word *alone* and use a reflexive pronoun with *by*.
1. We went there alone. (We went there by ourselves.)
2. She lives alone.
3. He has an old uncle who goes everywhere alone.
4. Do you like to go to the movies alone?
5. I never go out at night alone.
6. They eat lunch alone every day.
7. Do you and your brother like to play alone?
8. Do you ever swim alone?

D. Rewrite these sentences using the word *whose*.
1. To whom does this scarf belong? (Whose scarf is this?)
2. To whom does that lawn mower belong?
3. To whom does this car belong, you or her?
4. To whom does that coat belong, her or her sister?
5. To whom do these magazines belong?
6. To whom do these books belong?
7. To whom do those things belong?
8. To whom do those credit cards belong, you or your mother?

Reading and Conversation: A Smart Boy

William Henry Harrison, the ninth president of the United States, was born in a small town. As a young boy, he was very quiet and bashful. In fact, he was so quiet that many people thought he was stupid.

"It's a funny thing," William's mother said to him one day. "I know that you are a smart boy, but sometimes you let people think you are not so smart. I wonder why?"

The people of the town liked to play tricks on this boy who they thought was so stupid.

"Here, William," one of them would say. "Here is a nickel, and here is a dime. Which one do you want?"

William always chose the nickel, and all the people would laugh at him.

Finally, his mother took him aside and said to him, "William, why do you always choose the nickel instead of the dime? Don't you know that a dime is worth more than a nickel?"

"Certainly I know it," William answered slowly, "but if I choose the dime, then people won't play the trick on me anymore. Then I won't get any more nickels."

A. Comprehension and Conversation

1. Who was William Henry Harrison? Where was he born?
2. What kind of a boy was he?
3. What kind of a boy or girl were you?
4. What did William's mother wonder?
5. What was the trick that people played on William?
6. What did the people do when he chose the nickel? Why?
7. Why did he choose the nickel instead of the dime?
8. What is a *nickel?* A *dime?* What other coins do you know?
9. Do you know any people like William? Why do they act stupid when they are really smart?
10. Do you ever play tricks? What do you do?

B. Vocabulary

	Nouns	Verbs	Adjectives
meat	match	light	bashful
age	knife	burn	stupid
hand	nickel	hurt	
fire	dime	wash	
city	coin	be worth	*Adverbs*
box	grandparents	be related	finally
			anymore
			really

C. Expressions

Use each of these expressions in a sentence.
it's too late, in fact, a funny thing, let people think, play a trick.

D. Pronunciation Drill

p as in pie, happy, hope

part	pay	shampoo	up
pass	pear	surprise	shop
pause	permit	people	cup
park	pick	apple	sleep

unit thirteen

Dialogue

MS. NASH	Rolando, do you like to play baseball?
ROLANDO:	Yes, I do.
MS. NASH:	Are you on the school baseball team?
ROLANDO:	Yes, I am.
MS. NASH:	What position do you play?
ROLANDO:	I play first base.
MS. NASH:	Do you practice every day?
ROLANDO:	Yes, we do. During baseball season.
MS. NASH:	Did you practice last Saturday?
ROLANDO:	No, I didn't. I was sick that day.
MS. NASH:	When is the next game?
ROLANDO:	It's Saturday. We play the Lincoln Lions.
MS. NASH:	Can you bat well?
ROLANDO:	No, I can't. My batting average is .143.
MS. NASH:	That's not good?
ROLANDO:	No, it isn't.
MS. NASH:	I have never understood what a batting average is. Have you ever written about baseball, Rolando?
ROLANDO:	No, I haven't.
MS. NASH:	I think a good topic for your next composition would be an explanation of what a batting average is, don't you?
ROLANDO:	*(Glumly)* Yes, I do.

Answer these questions. Use short answers when it is possible.
1. Is Rolando on the school baseball team?
2. Are you on a school team?
2. Do you play any sport? Which one?
4. Is Rolando a pitcher?
5. What position do you play on your team?
6. When is baseball season in the United States?
7. Is baseball popular in your country? When is it played?

8. Do you think Mr. Nash's idea for a composition is a good one?
9. Do you know what a batting average is? Explain it to the class.

Grammar and Usage

1. Short Answers

We use short answers to answer simple questions. In these answers, we use a subject expressed by a pronoun and an auxiliary verb.

Do you speak English?	Can you write well?
Yes, I do.	Yes, I can.
No, I don't.	No, I can't.
Does John speak well?	Have you been to Chicago?
Yes, he does.	Yes, I have.
No, he doesn't.	No, I haven't.
Are you sick?	Will they come tomorrow?
Yes, I am.	Yes, they will.
No, I'm not.	No, they won't.

2. Sequence of Tenses

a. If the main verb of an English sentence is in the past tense, all other dependent verbs in the sentence are put in the past tense.

He says he is going to Chicago.
He *said* he *was going* to Chicago.
She says her father is ill.
She *said* her father *was* ill.

b. When part of the dependent verb is *can, may, will,* or *shall,* use those forms if the main verb is in the present tense. If the main verb is in the past tense, use their past forms *could, might, would,* and *should.*

He says he *can* go.
He said he *could* go.
They think they *may* leave on Thursday.
They thought they *might* leave on Thursday.
She says she *will* do it.
She said she *would* do it.

Exercises

A. Give affirmative short answers to these questions.
1. Do you wash your hair every day? (Yes, I do.)
2. Are there many pages in this book?
3. Do you sometimes go to the movies?
4. Did you take your medicine yesterday?
5. Was George Washington the first president of the United States?
6. Have you ever been to New York City?
7. Can you speak English?
8. Will you be in school next week?

B. Give negative short answers to these questions.
1. Do you wash dishes every day? (No, I don't.)
2. Are there eight days in a week?
3. Do you have four sisters?
4. Did you watch TV last night?
5. Was George Washington the second president of the United States?
6. Have you been to Hong Kong?
7. Can you speak Chinese?
8. Will you be in school on Sunday?

C. Change these sentences to the past tense and follow the rule of sequence of tenses.
1. She says she is busy. (She said she was busy.)
2. He says his name is Mario.
3. I hope they can go with us.
4. Do you know where they are?
5. It seems that we cannot do it.
6. Does she know what she will do?
7. I think he may change his mind about going.
8. What does the note say we can do?

D. Change these sentences to the present tense and follow the rule of sequence of tenses. Use contractions wherever possible.
1. He said he would be back soon. (He says he'll be back soon.)
2. She said her first name was Mary.
3. He hoped he could catch an early flight.

4. I told them I couldn't go.
5. She said she did not want to go.
6. I wondered if the blue hat might not be better with her coloring.
7. Was he sure that it was going to rain?
8. Did you think she was crying?

Reading and Conversation:
The Young Men and the Bull

Once upon a time, two young men were spending some time in the country. One day, while taking a walk together, they crossed a large field.

"Look out!" one of the young men shouted, because a bull suddenly appeared and began to chase them. Naturally they were frightened. They ran as fast as they could, but the bull kept chasing them.

Finally, one of the men climbed a tree. The other one jumped into a hole, but soon he came out of the hole again. Immediately the bull chased him back into the hole.

"Stay there," his friend shouted, but soon the man came out of the hole again, and again the bull chased him right back. This went on five or six more times.

Finally, the man in the tree got angry and shouted to his friend in the hole, "You fool! Stay in that hole for a while. Otherwise, this bull will keep us here all day!"

"That's easy for you to say," the other man said as he jumped one more time back into the hole, "but there happens to be a bear in this hole."

A. Comprehension and Conversation

1. Where were the two young men in this story? What were they doing?
2. What is a *bull?* Why did they run from the bull? Why were they frightened?
3. Where did the men go to try to escape the bull?
4. What happened when the man in the hole came out?
5. How often did this happen?
6. What would you do if you came upon a bull in a field?

7. Why was the man in the tree angry?
8. Why didn't the other man want to stay in the hole?
9. What is a *bear?* Why was this also a problem?
10. What would you do if you saw a bear? Would you be afraid?

B. Vocabulary

Nouns		Verbs		Adverbs
bear	bull	be back	continue	suddenly
note	field	cross	cry	immediately
fool	hole	shout	jump	
		chase		

C. Expressions

Use each of these expressions in a sentence.
the day after tomorrow, first name, once upon a time, Look out!, stay there, right back, that's easy for you to say, a while.

D. Pronunciation Drill

 as in <u>y</u>es, mill<u>i</u>on, amuse [əm<u>y</u>uwz]

yes	your	yellow	familiar
yet	young	use	New York
year	yesterday	Italian	million
you	yourself	useless	William

Robert Sietsema

unit fourteen

Dialogue

TOM: Ms. Nash, sometimes when I'm studying my English book I see explanations using the phrase *parts of speech.* I think I know all of the parts of speech, but I want to be certain.

MS. NASH: That's a good idea, Tom. Let's do it together, class. Jane, you start. Tell us about adjectives and adverbs.

JANE: An adjective is a word which modifies a noun. In the sentence "The young men walked slowly through the field," *young* is an adjective. It modifies the noun *men.* An adverb is a word which modifies a verb, an adjective, or another adverb. The word *slowly* in the sentence is an adverb. It modifies the verb *walked;* it tells how the men walked.

MS. NASH: Excellent, Jane. Now, Peter, tell us about nouns and verbs.

PETER: A noun is the name of a person, place, thing, or idea. Both *men* and *field* are nouns in the sentence above. *Men* is the subject of the sentence and *field* is the object of a preposition. Verbs are words that tell the action or the being of a noun. *Walked* is the verb in our sentence. It tells what the young men did.

MS. NASH: Peter said something about a preposition. Carol, do you know what a preposition is?

CAROL: Yes, I do. It's a word which links a noun or pronoun with the rest of the sentence, like *through* in the example. It helps describe time, place, or relationship. What about conjunctions, Ms. Nash. What are they?

MS. NASH: They are words which connect two or more words or ideas and show the relationship between them. Some examples are *and, but,* and *or.*

TOM: I think we're forgetting one part of speech.

MS. NASH: You're right, Tom. We are forgetting one. Do you know which one?

TOM: Yes, I do. It's pronouns. Pronouns are words used in place of nouns or phrases so that we don't have to repeat them. Some examples are *we, them, who, that,* and *which.*

Answer these questions:
1. What is an adjective? Give an example of a sentence and tell which word is the adjective.
2. What is an adverb? Give an example of a sentence and tell which word is the adverb.
3. What is a noun? Which are the nouns in this sentence: "The old scientist came into the laboratory with her assistant."
4. What is a verb? What does it do in a sentence? What is the verb in the sentence in question 3?
5. What is a preposition? What does it do in a sentence? What are the prepositions in the sentence in question 3?
6. What are conjunctions? What do they do? Give some examples of conjunctions.
7. What are pronouns? How are they used in sentences? How many pronouns can you name?

Identify the parts of speech in each of these sentences:
8. She usually asks him for the keys to the car.
9. I want to go to the movies or to the new Chinese restaurant.
10. Where do you and your brother want me to put this baby gorilla which I brought you?

Grammar and Usage

1. Adverbs

a. Many adverbs are formed by adding *-ly* to an adjective.
rapid – rapidly, slow – slowly

b. Some words may be used as both adjectives and adverbs with no change in form.
> *fast, hard, late, early*
> She is a *hard* worker. She works *hard.*
> I am a *fast* walker. I walk *fast.*

c. The comparative form of adverbs is formed (see also Lesson 4 for the comparison of adjectives) by adding *-er* to one-syllable and some two-syllable adverbs. For some two-syllable adverbs and for adverbs with more than two syllables, use *more.* As with the comparative form of adjectives, this form is always followed by *than.*
> *soon – sooner*
> *early – earlier*
> *quickly – more quickly*
> *merrily – more merrily*
> She came *earlier* than we.
> He walks *more rapidly* than I.

2. Comparison of Equality

A comparison of equality with both adverbs and adjectives uses the form *as . . . as.*
> *Adjective:* She is *as* tall *as* her brother.
> We are *as* smart *as* our parents.
> *Adverb:* I came *as* soon *as* I could.
> He ran *as* rapidly *as* his sister.

3. Nouns and Verbs with the Same Form

Some words serve as both nouns and verbs with no change in form. The following is a partial list of some common words which may be used as nouns or as verbs:

taste	smell	cost	cross
cry	curse	cut	design
dress	end	fool	guarantee
hope	wish	need	stay

> These apples *smell* bad.
> The *smell* of the ammonia was strong.

He has a bad *cough.*
    I hope you don't *cough* all night.
Our vacations always *end* too early.
    We will leave at the *end* of this month.

Exercises

A. Supply the adverbial form of the adjective in parentheses.
1. He said he would certainly do it. (certain)
2. I will _____ do it for you. (glad)
3. She spoke _____ about her work. (happy)
4. We arrived _____. (early)
5. They arrived _____. (late)
6. The teacher sometimes speaks very _____. (rapid)
7. Will you finish your work _____? (quick)
8. Can you read this writing _____? (easy)

B. Some of these sentences require adjectives, and others require adverbs. Supply the correct form of the word in parentheses.
1. He appears to be a happy person. (happy)
2. They lived together _____. (happy)
3. I always do my work _____. (careful)
4. She is a _____ student. (careful)
5. The old man's face remained _____. (blank)
6. He looked at me _____. (blank)
7. Do you study _____? (private)
8. Do you take _____ lessons? (private)

C. Express the words in parentheses in the correct comparative form.
1. Ed walks more rapidly than I. (rapid)
2. He goes there _____ his brothers. (often)
3. We walked _____ was necessary. (far)
4. She came _____ anyone expected. (early)
5. She left _____ she had planned. (late)
6. Can you run _____ your friend? (fast)

7. Does he play the piano _____ his teacher? (beautiful)
8. Do you think Ms. Nash speaks _____ Mr. Schwartz? (slow)

D. Introduce the form *as . . . as* into the following sentences. Use the words in parentheses.
1. He is as tall as his brother. (tall)
2. She comes here _____ I do. (often)
3. They did not arrive _____ we expected. (early)
4. Can you run _____ your sister? (fast)
5. Is your aunt _____ your uncle? (bashful)
6. Did it work _____ you thought? (easily)
7. This light is _____ that one. (bright)
8. The dog isn't _____ the cat. (quiet)

Reading and Conversation: Paderewski's Pupil

Ignace Jan Paderewski, the famous pianist, was once walking down the street of a small town in Poland. He passed a house and saw a sign hanging outside which said
          D. Bielski   Piano Lessons $25
Inside, someone was playing one of Chopin's nocturnes. Paderewski stopped and listened. The playing, however, was very bad. In fact, it was so bad that Paderewski felt it was an insult to the memory of Chopin. Finally, he walked up to the door and knocked. When Miss Bielski herself answered the door, Paderewski introduced himself and explained to her that he had listened to her play. He also said that, if she wished him to do so, he would gladly play the nocturne for her in the way that a pianist should play it. Miss Bielski was very happy to hear this and invited Paderewski to come in. Paderewski entered and for half an hour played several of Chopin's pieces.

About a year later, Paderewski was in the same town again and was walking down the same street. Coming to the same house again, he now saw this new sign hanging outside:

D. Bielski   (Pupil of Paderewski)
Piano Lessons $50

A. Comprehension and Conversation

1. Who was Paderewski? Do you know where he was from?
2. What did he see while walking down a street? What did it say?
3. What was happening inside the house? Who was responsible?
4. What did Paderewski decide to do?
5. Was Miss Bielski happy when he played her piano?
6. How long did he play? How do you think Miss Bielski felt?
7. What did Paderewski see when he returned to the town?
8. Why did Miss Bielski raise the cost of piano lessons from twenty-five dollars to fifty dollars?
9. Do you play the piano? Would you like to play it? Do you enjoy listening to the piano?
10. What other famous pianists can you name? What other composers (besides Chopin)?

B. Vocabulary

Nouns		*Verbs*		*Other*
explanation	action	modify	connect	private
being	example	link	enter	adverbial
rest	relationship	taste	introduce	besides
face	pianist	cross	invite	
nocturne	insult	hang	knock	
pupil	piece	design	repeat	
composer		expect	appear	

C. Expressions

Use each of these expressions in a sentence.
now tell us, in place of, half an hour, play the piano, about a year later.

D. Pronunciation Drill

ɑ   as in army, hot, father, guard

army	problem	park	father
honest	far	farm	on
are	not	hard	novel
popular	hot	upon	dark

United States Postal Service

unit fifteen

Dialogue

PAUL: Give me a roll of first-class stamps, please.

CLERK: Here you are. That will be twenty dollars. Anything else?

PAUL: Yes, I want some post cards and some foreign airmail stamps. I want to send some letters to South America.

CLERK: Just a moment, I'll look up the rate for an airmail letter to South America.

PAUL: Can you tell me how much it will cost to send a package to Colombia? I also want to know how long it will take.

CLERK: You have to have the package with you so that I can weigh it. I would have to know how much it weighs before I could tell you the cost. It will take about a week, if you send it the fastest way.

PAUL: Do you insure packages?

CLERK: Yes, all you have to do is declare the value of the package and decide how much insurance you want. It only takes a minute to complete the forms, and the rates are reasonable.

PAUL: Is there a way that I can be sure that the people in South America have received my package?

CLERK: The post office rarely loses packages. You can, however, request a return receipt. With a return receipt, when the person who delivers your package gives it to your friend, your friend has to sign for it. We then notify you that he or she has it.

Answer these questions:
1. Where does this conversation take place? Between what two people?
2. What three items does the customer want to buy?
3. What does *first class* mean? *Air mail?* What is a *post card?*

4. Do you usually send your letters by first-class mail? Do you sent post cards?
5. How long does it take to send a letter from the United States to your country? To Colombia?
6. Why would Paul want to insure his package?
7. Why would Paul (or anyone) want a return receipt?
8. How much is the equivalent of a first-class stamp in your country today?
9. How long does it take to send a letter from one city to another in your country?
10. When was the last time you had to go to the post office? What did you have to do there?

Grammar and Usage

1. *Have to*

a. *Have to (has to)* plus the verb expresses necessity or strong obligation.
>I *have to study* tonight.
>He *has to work* tonight.

b. The past tense of *have to* is *had to.*
>I *had to study* last night.
>He *had to work* last night.

Had to is also the past tense of *must.*
>I *must* study tonight.
>I *had to* study last night.

c. The negative and question forms of *have to* are regular.
>I do not (don't) have to work today.
>I will not (won't) have to work tomorrow.
>I have not (haven't) had to work all week.
>Do you have to work today?
>Will you have to work tomorrow?
>Have you had to work this week?

2. *It takes*

It takes is an idiomatic expression which we use to express the time which is necessary to complete an action. *It takes* is always followed by an infinitive.

It takes me two hours *to complete* my homework.
It took me three hours *to drive* home last night.
Will it take you long *to get* ready?

Exercises

A. Supply the correct form of *have to*.
  1. He has to work tonight.
  2. I _____ get up every morning at six o'clock.
  3. She _____ go to the doctor's office yesterday.
  4. _____ you _____ get up early yesterday morning?
  5. They _____ stay after school every day last week.
  6. You _____ stay home tomorrow to wait for the furniture delivery.
  7. _____ Jim _____ visit his aunt and uncle next month?
  8. We _____ finish this exercise today.

B. Change *must* to *have to* in each of these sentences.
  1. We must go to the hospital. (We have to go to the hospital.)
  2. I must take this package to the post office.
  3. The clerk must insure it.
  4. You must buy some stamps.
  5. We must get up early tomorrow.
  6. Must we wait on this corner for the bus?
  7. Must he give you a receipt?
  8. Must she come with us?

C. Change these sentences to the negative form.
  1. I have to go to the post office. (I don't have to go to the post office.)
  2. You have to send it by first-class mail.
  3. She has to give you a receipt.
  4. They will have to go to New York.
  5. You'll have to wear your warm coat.
  6. I'll have to wear mine, too.
  7. We had to take an exam yesterday.
  8. He had to wait there for three days.

D. Repeat Exercise C changing the sentences to simple questions.
  1. I have to go to the post office. (Do I have to go to the post office?)

E. Repeat Exercise C changing the sentences to questions beginning with *why*.
   1. I have to go to the post office. (Why do I have to go to the post office?)

F. Rewrite the following sentences using some form of the idiomatic expression *it takes*.
   1. I can walk there in twenty minutes. (It takes me twenty minutes to walk there.)
   2. He can get there by train in three hours.
   3. A first-class letter will arrive in a week.
   4. I did the work in twelve hours.
   5. She gets there by bus in thirty minutes.
   6. She walked there in half an hour.
   7. We finished it in five minutes.
   8. I will find it in about thirty minutes.

Reading and Conversation: *To get*

Instead of a reading in this lesson, we will have an explanation of the many uses of the verb *to get*. Expressions with *to get* fall into four main categories:
   1. used with the sense of *to arrive*.
      We *got home* at six o'clock last night.
      It will take the package a week *to get* there.
      This train *gets* to Atlanta at two-thirty p.m.
      I want *to get* to school on time today.
   2. used with almost any adjective, with the meaning of *to become*.
      She *got sick* after work yesterday.
      I *get hungry* every day around five o'clock.
      They *got tired* from all the hard work.
      If you play in the mud, you'll *get dirty*. *(muddy)*
   3. used in everyday expressions.
      I *get up* every morning at six o'clock.
      Where do you *get on* your bus?
      I *get off* my bus at 56th Street.
   4. used in special expressions.
      How are you *getting along* in school this year?
      If your daughter hits another child, don't let her *get away with* it.
      I know you are sad, but I hope you'll *get over* the death of your cat.

A. Comprehension and Conversation

1. What time do you get home from school every day?
2. What time do you get up in the morning?
3. Did you get sick at all last year?
4. Do you get tired if you have to walk too far?
5. How are you getting along in this class?
6. If you don't do your homework, does your teacher let you get away with it?
7. What do you do when you get hungry? Tired? Sad? Thirsty?
8. Do you ever get nervous before an examination?
9. How long does it take you to get to your friend's house?
10. In your city, do riders pay the fare when they get on the bus or when they got off the bus?

B. Vocabulary

Nouns		*Verbs*	*Adjectives*
stamp	post card	insure	first-class
rate	package	weigh	airmail
death	insurance	declare	reasonable
letter	customer	lose	idiomatic
corner	expression	notify	thirsty
doctor	hospital	request	nervous
return receipt			

Adverbs
rarely

C. Expressions

Use each of these expressions in a sentence.
just a moment, it only takes a minute, getting along in school, get away with it.

D. Pronunciation Drill

k as in cha<u>r</u>ac<u>t</u>er, Ameri<u>c</u>an, stea<u>k</u>

can	climb	keep	like
come	coffee	school	pick
cut	cough	o'clock	took
could	kill	picture	walk
queen	check	clock	instruction

Florida News Bureau Department of Commerce

unit sixteen

Dialogue

MS. NASH: Teresa, if you close your book, you'll be able to hear me. I think it is distracting you. Thank you. Now, Teresa, if today were a holiday, where would you go?

TERESA: If today were a holiday, I would go to the beach.

MS. NASH: Louis, if you sit up straight in your seat, you will be able to pay attention to the lesson. Good. Now, Louis, if you studied English harder, would you learn it more rapidly?

LOUIS: Yes, Ms. Nash, if I studied English harder, I'd learn it more rapidly.

MS. NASH: If you knew English well, Grace, what North American authors would you like to read?

GRACE: If I knew English well, I'd like to read some modern writers, like John Updike, Kurt Vonnegut, Jr., and Joyce Carol Oates.

MS. NASH: If you were a millionaire, George, what would you do?

GEORGE: If I were a millionaire, I would take a trip around the world.

MS. NASH: What about you, Peter? If you were a millionaire, what would you do? *(There is no answer. Peter seems to be deep in thought.)* Come on, Peter, if you pay attention and think, you'll have an answer. You have said nothing.

PETER: That's exactly what I would do if I were a millionaire, Ms. Nash—nothing at all.

Answer these questions:
1. If today were a holiday, where would you go?
2. If you study hard for your examinations, what will happen?

3. If you stay up all night, what will happen to you in the morning?
4. If you had more practice in conversation, would you be able to speak English better?
5. If you won a free trip to any city in the United States, where would you go?
6. If you eat too much at dinner tonight, how will you feel?
7. If you were in Europe right now, what countries would you like to visit?
8. If you were a millionaire, what would you do?
9. What does Peter say he would do if he were a millionaire?
10. What authors would Grace like to read if she knew English well? What authors would you like to read if you knew English well?

Grammar and Usage

Conditional Forms 1

A conditional sentence is one containing two clauses, one main or independent and one dependent. The dependent clause almost always begins with *if.*

If he comes, I will (I'll) speak to him.
If I knew her, I would (I'd) ask her to come.

a. *Future-possible conditions.* In this type of condition, we use the present tense in the *if* clause and the future tense in the main clause. These sentences always describe some possible future action which may or may not result.

If John *studies,* he *will pass* the exam.
If Teresa *closes* her book, she*'ll be able* to hear her teacher.

b. *Present-unreal conditions.* In this second type of condition, we use the past tense in the *if* clause and *would, could, should,* or *might* as the auxiliary verb in the main clause.

If John *studied,* he *would pass* the exam.
If Teresa *closed* her book, she*'d be able* to hear her teacher.

These sentences suggest a situation which is unreal or contrary to fact. Thus, John does not study, but *if he stud-*

ied, he would pass the exam. Teresa's book is open, but *if she closed it,* she would be able to hear Ms. Nash.

If the present-unreal conditions contain the verb *to be,* we use the form *were* for all the persons.

I were	we were
you were	you were
he were	
she were	they were
it were	

Exercises

A. Complete these future-possible sentences.
1. If you hurry, you will finish on time. (finish)
2. If he _____ on time, he can go to the movies with us. (come)
3. If I _____ time, I'll go with you. (have)
4. If the teacher helps him, he _____ much faster. (learn)
5. If she practices more, she _____ English better. (speak)
6. If I see Henry, I _____ him your message. (give)
7. If you _____ slowly, you won't have an accident. (drive)
8. If I _____ the book, I'll give it to you. (find)

B. Complete these present-unreal sentences.
1. If she were here, she would explain it to us. (explain)
2. If today _____ a holiday, I'd go to the beach. (be)
3. If I _____ time, I'd study more. (have)
4. If we had the money, we _____ a trip to Europe. (take)
5. If Louis _____ more grammar, he'd make fewer mistakes. (know)
6. If I went to bed earlier, I _____ not _____ so tired. (feel)
7. If you had the money, _____ you _____ a trip around the world? (take)
8. If I were you, I _____ not _____ anything to her about it. (say)

C. Change these sentences from future-possible to present-unreal.

1. If she tries hard, she'll find another job. (If she tried hard, she'd find another job.)
2. If you come early, you can help us.
3. If I'm not busy, I'll go to the movies with you.
4. If the weather is good, we'll take a walk.
5. If he has more money, he'll buy a car.
6. If you turn out the light, we'll be in the dark.
7. If he eats less and exercises more, he will lose weight.
8. If we work hard, we shall succeed.

Reading and Conversation:
The Popularity of the Elephant

One day a lot of the forest animals came together to talk about the popularity of the elephant. They all agreed that the elephant was the most popular animal in the forest, but not one of them could explain this.

The giraffe said, "If the elephant had a long neck like mine, then it would be easy to understand his popularity. He would be the tallest animal in the forest."

The peacock said, "If he had my beautiful tail, it would be easy to understand. He would be the most beautiful animal in the forest."

The rabbit said, "If he could run as fast as I, it would be easy to understand. He would be the fastest animal in the forest."

The bear said, "If he were as strong as I, it would be easy to understand. He would be the strongest animal in the forest."

At this moment, the elephant himself appeared. He was larger and stronger than any of the other animals, and he was also better in many other ways. But he was always quiet and modest about his many accomplishments. This was the real explanation for his popularity.

A. Comprehension and Conversation

1. What were the animals talking about? Why do you think they were talking about this?
2. What did they all agree on?
3. Do you think that all of your friends would agree who was the most popular person?

4. What did the giraffe say about the elephant's popularity?
5. What did the peacock say about the elephant's popularity?
6. What did the rabbit say about the elephant's popularity?
7. What did the bear say about the elephant's popularity?
8. What do you have to say about the elephant's popularity?
9. What do you think of people who are quiet and modest?
10. What do you think of people who are proud and who talk about their accomplishments all the time?

B. Vocabulary

	Nouns	*Verbs*	*Adjectives*
tail	millionaire	distract	conditional
rabbit	thought	sit up	straight
author	elephant	pay attention	free
neck	accomplishment	suggest	deep
peacock	holiday	understand	real
giraffe	situation	agree	unreal
beach	accident		modest
forest	popularity		proud

C. Expressions

Use each of these expressions in a sentence.
a trip around the world, deep in thought, come on, nothing at all, contrary to fact.

D. Pronunciation Drill

When -s (or -es) is added to any word which ends in a voiced sound, the -s becomes voiced and is pronounced like z.

goes	knows	countries	bags
pays	runs	stories	dimes
comes	rains	shoes	guns
finds	snows	papers	towns

Air France

unit seventeen

Dialogue

MS. NASH: Class, yesterday we learned about the future-possible and the present-unreal conditional forms. Today, we're going to learn about the past-unreal conditional form. Teresa, I'm going to ask you the same question I asked you yesterday but in a different form. If yesterday had been a holiday, where would you have gone?

TERESA: If yesterday had been a holiday, Ms. Nash, I would have gone to the beach.

MS. NASH: Good. Louis, if you had been in Europe last summer, what countries would you have visited?

LOUIS: If I had been in Europe last summer, I'd have visited France, Spain, and perhaps Italy.

MS. NASH: Grace, if you had had nothing to do last night, where would you have gone?

GRACE: If I had had nothing to do last night, I probably would have gone to the ballet. I love good dancing.

MS. NASH: If you had been born in Germany, George, what language would you have learned as a child?

GEORGE: If I had been born in Germany, I would have learned German as a child because in Germany everyone speaks German.

MS. NASH: Peter, if you had been born in China, what language would you have learned as a child?

PETER: If I had been born in China, I'd have learned Chinese as a child, but I'm glad I was born here, Ms. Nash.

MS. NASH: Why is that, Peter?

PETER: Because my parents only speak English. It would be very confusing at home if I only spoke Chinese.

Answer these questions:
1. If yesterday had been a holiday, where would you have gone?

2. If yesterday had been Sunday, would you have gone to school?
3. What did Ms. Nash say the class was going to study today? What did the class study yesterday?
4. What countries would Louis have visited if he had been in Europe last summer? What countries would you have visited if you had been in Europe last summer?
5. If you had had a vacation last week, what would you have done?
6. What is a *ballet?* Have you ever seen one? Would you like to see a ballet?
7. Why is Peter happy that he was not born in China?
8. If you had been born in Canada, what languages might you have learned as a child? In France? In Japan?
9. What would have happened if you had studied harder for your last examination?
10. What would you have done if it had snowed yesterday?

Grammar and Usage

Conditional Forms 2

In past-unreal conditions, we use the past perfect tense in the *if* clause and *would have, could have,* or *might have* in the main clause.

> If John had studied, he would have passed.
> If yesterday had been a holiday, I would have gone to the beach.

Note that these conditions are similar to present-unreal conditions in that they indicate a situation which is unreal or contrary to fact. Thus, John did not study, but *if he had studied,* he would have passed. Yesterday was not a holiday, but *if it had been a holiday,* I would have gone to the beach.

Present Tense after *when, until, as soon as*

We learned that in future-possible conditions we use the present tense in the *if* clause. Similarly, after the subordinate conjunctions *until, when, as soon as, before,* and *unless,* we also use the present tense.

> If he *comes,* I will tell him.
> When he *comes,* I will tell him.
> As soon as he *comes,* I will tell him.
> I will wait here until he *comes.*

Exercises

A. Supply the correct form in these past-unreal sentences.
1. He would have done it if you had asked him. (ask)
2. She _____ if you had invited her. (go)
3. She would have waited if she _____ you were here. (know)
4. If I _____ the tree in a better place, it would've grown. (plant)
5. If I had known it was going to rain, I _____ my umbrella. (take)
6. If Henry _____ here, he might have helped us. (be)
7. If I _____ your number, I could've called you. (have)
8. If I had been in your place, I _____ not _____. (go)

B. Change these future-possible conditions first to present-unreal conditions, then to past-unreal conditions.
1. If it rains, I won't go. (If it rained, I wouldn't go. If it had rained, I wouldn't have gone.)
2. If she studies, she'll pass.
3. If I don't have to study, I'll go with you.
4. If you water the flowers regularly, they will bloom.
5. If this is theirs, I'll return it to them.
6. If it snows, I'll stay home.
7. If it rains, will you stay home, too?
8. If we plant the tree there, will it grow?

C. Supply the correct verb form.
1. We can talk to them tomorrow when they come. (come)
2. I'll wait here until she _____. (get back)
3. If it _____ tomorrow, we'll stay home. (rain)
4. If it _____ not _____, we'll go to the beach. (rain)
5. I'll let you know as soon as she _____. (call)
6. If I had any money, I _____ it to you. (lend)
7. Please notify me when the meeting _____ over. (be)
8. I'm not going unless you _____, too. (go)

Reading and Conversation:
The Farmer and the Apple Tree

A poor farmer once had a friend who was famous for the wonderful apple trees which she grew. The farmer went to visit his friend one fine day in the spring. As the farmer was about to leave, his friend said, "Here is a young apple tree. I want you to take it home and plant it. I want you and your family to enjoy it."

The farmer was pleased. "Thank you very much," he said. "I know this tree will bear fine apples."

But when the farmer got home, he did not know where to plant it. He was afraid that if he planted the tree near the road, strangers would steal the fruit. If he planted the tree in one of his fields, his neighbors would come at night and steal some of the apples. If he planted the tree near his house, his children would take the fruit. Finally, he planted the tree deep in his woods, where no one could see it. But, naturally, without sunlight and proper soil, the tree soon died.

Later that year, the friend who had given the farmer the tree went over to his farm to visit. Naturally, she inquired about the tree.

"Why did you plant the tree in such a poor place?" she asked, puzzled.

"What's the difference?" the farmer said angrily. "If I had planted the tree near the road, strangers would have stolen the fruit. If I had planted the tree in one of my fields, my neighbors would have come at night and stolen some of the apples. If I had planted it near my house, my own children would have taken the fruit."

"Yes," said the friend. "But at least someone could have enjoyed the fruit. Now, by your foolish action, you have robbed everyone of the fruit, and you have also destroyed a good tree."

A. Comprehension and Conversation

1. What was the friend of the farmer famous for? When did he visit his friend?
2. What did the friend give the farmer? What did she tell him to do with the gift?

3. Why was the farmer afraid to plant the tree near the road?
4. What did he think would happen if he planted it in one of his fields? Near the house?
5. Where did he finally plant the tree? Why?
6. If the farmer had planted the tree in a better place, what would have happened? Why?
7. What happened when the farmer's friend went over to visit him later in the year? What did she ask him?
8. How did he explain his actions? What was her response?
9. What should the farmer have done? What would you have done?
10. Do all trees grow easily? What is the proper season of the year to plant trees? When do they bear fruit?

B. Vocabulary

Nouns		Verbs		Adjectives
ballet	dancing	grow	destroy	different
flower	response	die	inquire	fine
gift	sunlight	bear	rob	proper
soil	apple tree	plant		foolish
woods				

Adverbs
naturally

C. Expressions

Use each of these expressions in a sentence.
nothing to do, What's the difference?, deep in the woods.

D. Pronunciation Drill

When -s (or -es) is added to any word which ends in an unvoiced sound, the -s remains unvoiced and is pronounced like s.

takes	writes	parts	students
likes	hats	helps	cents
books	speaks	walks	waits
picks	habits	works	costs

American Airlines

unit eighteen

Dialogue

AGENT: May I help you?

JOHN: I'd like to buy a ticket to Washington, D.C., please.

AGENT: When will you be going, sir?

JOHN: I intend going next Monday. What flights do you have on that day?

AGENT: Let me see. *(She consults her desk-top computer.)* We have two flights on Monday, and both have seats available. One is at eight-forty a.m., and the other is at seven forty-five p.m.

JOHN: I'll take the morning flight, please. It's more convenient for me.

AGENT: Will that be smoking or nonsmoking?

JOHN: Nonsmoking, please.

AGENT: Will you be traveling first class this trip?

JOHN: No, I want a coach seat, please. By the way, is there a meal on this flight?

AGENT: Yes, the computer shows that you'll be served breakfast on this flight.

JOHN: Good, I might not have time to have breakfast at home.

AGENT: Will you be returning with us, sir? I mean, do you want a round-trip ticket?

JOHN: No, I'll be driving back. I enjoy traveling by air, but driving is more fun.

Answer these questions:
1. Where does this dialogue take place? Between what two people?
2. Where does John want to go? When?
3. Why is he flying in the morning?
4. What is the difference between first class and coach?
5. Have you ever flown? When? Where? Did you enjoy it?

6. What's the difference between the *smoking* and the *nonsmoking* sections on an airplane?
7. How is John returning? Why?
8. Do you enjoy traveling by plane? Do you enjoy driving more?
9. What does *a.m.* mean? What does *p.m.* mean?
10. What is a *desk-top computer?* Why did the agent consult hers?

Grammar and Usage

Gerunds

a. Gerunds are nouns which are formed from verbs. They always end in *-ing* (traveling, driving, eating, flying). They are used as subjects, direct objects of verbs, and objects of prepositions.

b. Certain verbs in English are always followed by gerunds and never by infinitives. These verbs are *enjoy, mind, avoid, consider, appreciate, finish, deny, admit,* and *risk.*
He has finished *taking* lessons.
Do you mind *waiting* a few minutes?

c. Some verbs, like *begin, continue, hate, prefer, like,* and *intend,* may be followed by gerunds or infinitives.
He likes to *study* with us.
He likes *studying* with us.
He prefers *to go* to Washington.
He prefers *going* to Washington.

Exercises

A. Supply the gerund form of the verb in parentheses.
1. Do you mind waiting a few minutes? (wait)
2. We are considering _____ a computer. (buy)
3. He enjoys _____ more than _____. (drive, fly)
4. She has finished _____ piano lessons. (take)
5. They admitted _____ the money. (steal)
6. I couldn't avoid _____ on the icy walk. (fall)
7. Are you going to risk _____ in this weather? (drive)
8. The letter said, "We shall appreciate _____ from you at once." (hear)

B. Complete these sentences using the verbs in parentheses first in the infinitive form, then in the gerund form.
   1. They will continue _____ in our class. (study) (They will continue *to study* in our class. They will continue *studying* in our class.)
   2. Do you prefer _____ in the morning or in the evening? (fly)
   3. I'll continue _____ to her. (write)
   4. My sister has begun _____ English classes. (take)
   5. She always hated _____ that kind of work. (do)
   6. Joe will start _____ in the new building on Monday. (work)
   7. I always liked _____ early in the morning. (get up)
   8. Are you going to continue _____? (smoke)

C. Supply the correct infinitive or gerund.
   1. John enjoys traveling by plane. (travel)
   2. I want _____ a trip next week. (take)
   3. He hopes _____ for Chicago tomorrow. (leave)
   4. We are considering _____ this lesson soon. (stop)
   5. Do you deny _____ that the bank was going to be robbed? (know)
   6. She asked me _____ for her. (wait)
   7. Are you going _____ to another city? (move)
   8. I hope it is going to stop _____ soon. (rain)

Reading and Conversation:
Robert Bruce and the Spider

Robert Bruce was a famous Scottish general. In the early fourteenth century, he tried to drive the English out of Scotland, but he was unsuccessful; the English were too strong. Soon he was spending all his time running away and hiding.

One day, he lay in his cave thinking of the sad state of Scotland. A spider began to make a web above his head. Simply to pass the time, Bruce broke the web. Immediately the spider began to make a new one. Six times Bruce broke the web, and six times the spider immediately made a new one. Bruce was surprised at this. He told himself that he would break the web a seventh time. If the spider made a new one, it would be a good lesson to him, for like the spider, he had been defeated six times. Bruce then broke the web. Again the spider made a new one.

From this simple fact, Bruce became encouraged. He again got an army together. This time he was successful in driving the English out of Scotland.

A. Comprehension and Conversation

1. Who was Robert Bruce?
2. What was he trying to do in the fourteenth century? Was he successful? Why?
3. What did he spend his time doing?
4. What did he notice while lying in his cave? What was he thinking about while he was lying there?
5. What was the spider's reaction to what Bruce had done? How often did this activity repeat itself?
6. What lesson did Bruce learn from this incident?
7. Have you ever learned a lesson from watching an animal? Describe it.
8. What other famous generals do you know?
9. Where is Scotland? Is it a small country? What languages are spoken there?
10. What is a *spider?* Is it large or small? Where do spiders live?

B. Vocabulary

Nouns			*Verbs*	
spider	flight	intend	consider	drive out
agent	coach	consult	avoid	run away
step	web	bother	risk	defeat
cave	century	smoke	hate	continue
desk-top		serve	break	appreciate
computer		admit		
round-trip				
ticket				

C. Expressions

Use each of these expressions in a sentence.
let me see, at night, by the way, right now, sad state, simple fact.

D. Pronunciation Drill

In which of the following words is the final -*s* pronounced like *z*, and in which is it pronounced like *s*?

books	comes	caves	pleases
eggs	goes	lessons	breaks
does	minds	sits	webs
takes	berths	sees	drives

© *Margot Granitsas*

unit nineteen

Dialogue

CRISTINA: Ms. Nash, may books be taken from the school library?

MS. NASH: Yes, Cristina, books may be taken from this library and from the public library over on Elm Street.

CRISTINA: How long may the books be kept?

MS. NASH: I think the borrowing period is three weeks. Yes, I'm sure it is. Books from both libraries may be kept for three weeks.

CRISTINA: Ms. Nash, can you tell me where typing paper, envelopes, ink, and pencils can be bought?

MS. NASH: Those items may be bought in a stationery store, Cristina. There's one in the Elmwood Shopping Center. Let's all help Cristina learn where to buy things in town, class. Jennifer, where can Cristina find good clothing at low prices?

JENNIFER: Good clothing can be found at Susan's, a small shop in the shopping center, Ms. Nash.

MS. NASH: What about restaurants, William? Where can good food for low prices be found?

WILLIAM: Good food can be found at Pedro's, a Cuban-Chinese restaurant downtown.

MS. NASH: What about books and magazines? Where can they be bought?

PETER: Anderson's is a good newsstand on Oak Street. Out-of-town newspapers and European magazines can be bought there. New books can be bought at a discount at Beck's near the newsstand.

Answer these questions:
1. What does Cristina want to know about the school library?

2. May books be borrowed from your school library? How long may they be kept?
3. What kind of books can be found in the library in your city?
4. Where is the nearest public library?
5. In what kind of store can men's suits and shirts be bought? What is a good one?
6. In what kind of store can women's dresses and blouses be bought? What is a good one?
7. What did Ms. Nash ask William? What was his response?
8. What is your favorite restaurant?
9. Where can newspapers and magazines be bought in your city?
10. Where can books be bought in your city?

Grammar and Usage

1. Special Passive Forms

a. The passive voice of verbs containing the auxiliaries *have to, can, must,* and *may* is formed by adding *be* to the past participle of the main verb. The passive form of infinitives is formed the same way.
He has to do it today.
It *has to be done* today.
He can bring it tomorrow.
It *can be brought* tomorrow.
You may borrow the books.
The books *may be borrowed.*

b. We form the passive voice of the various continuous tenses by using *to be* in its continuous form as an auxiliary.

Present Continuous: He is writing the letter now.
The letter *is being written* now.
Past Continuous: They were reading those books yesterday.
Those books *were being read* yesterday.

2. Gerunds with Prepositions

Since gerunds function as nouns, they are often used after prepositions.

She is fond *of swimming.*
They want more practice *in speaking* English.

Exercises

A. Change these sentences to the passive voice.
1. He is writing a letter to the department store. (A letter is being written to the department store.)
2. They are sending the books today.
3. They were repairing the piano.
4. I was planning the work.
5. She is bringing the papers now.
6. The spider is catching a fly.
7. We are forming new sentences.
8. Are you planting the tree today?

B. Change these sentences to the passive voice.
1. She can do it today. (It can be done today.)
2. She can't do it today.
3. We must bring it to him today.
4. You must write the letter at once.
5. You may put this in my office.
6. We may borrow books from the library.
7. We should do it right away.
8. We shouldn't do it yet.
9. We have to do it right away.
10. He has to bring it today.
11. They have to finish the work today.
12. We ought to buy the tickets now.
13. They ought to leave the animals in the forest.
14. Does she have to do it right away?
15. We had to hand in our papers yesterday.
16. He had to finish the test quickly.

C. Supply the correct preposition and the gerund form of the verb in parentheses.
1. I am fond of flying in airplanes. (fly)

2. They were not interested _____ about my trip. (hear)
3. I was afraid _____ the directions. (lose)
4. There was no danger _____ the dog there. (leave)
5. You should have no difficulty _____ him. (find)
6. We need more practice _____ English. (speak)
7. I am very fond _____. (swim)
8. Are you interested _____ that new movie? (see)

Reading and Conversation: The Love Letter

One day, after receiving a letter from her boyfriend, a young woman called him to say how much she enjoyed the letter.

"It was wonderful, all those beautiful things you said."

"I meant every one of them," the young man replied.

Among other things, he wrote that he loved her and that he thought she was wonderful. The letter was full of poetic thoughts.

"The part I loved most was when you said that in order to be with me, you would suffer the greatest difficulties and face the greatest dangers that anyone could imagine."

"Yes, it's true," he said. "In fact, to spend one minute with you I would climb the highest mountain in the world, I would swim the widest river, I would enter the deepest forest and fight the fiercest animals with my bare hands.

He had written all this in his letter, too.

"There's just one part of the letter that puzzles me," the young woman then said.

"What's that?"

"You signed your name and then added a postscript. Do you remember?"

"Of course. It was important, but I forgot to put it in the body of the letter."

"Your postscript says, 'By the way, I'll be over to see you on Wednesday night—if it doesn't rain.'"

A. Comprehension and Conversation

1. What two people are talking on the phone?
2. Why were they talking? Who called whom?

3. What kind of letter did the young man write? What kind of thoughts did he express?
4. What did he mean when he said he would "face the greatest dangers"?
5. What kind of dangers was he prepared to face?
6. What is a *postscript?* What did the postscript to this letter say?
7. Why is his postscript amusing and puzzling to her?
8. Have you ever read a love letter in a book? What did it say?
9. What is the highest mountain in the world? In the United States? In your country?
10. What do you think of the poetic language which the young man used in his letter?

B. Vocabulary

Nouns		Verbs	Adjectives
love letter	ink	borrow	special
postscript	river	take	wild
typing paper	forest	puzzle	poetic
envelopes	suit	keep	bare
mountain	shirt		fierce
stationery store	dress		
clothing	thought		
restaurant	blouse		
price			

C. Expressions

Use each of these expressions in a sentence.
near the . . . , at once, with my bare hands, of course, body of the letter.

D. Pronunciation Drill

dʒ as in joy, cordial, large

joke	agent	jump	just
soldier	subject	large	John
page	Japan	strange	James
encourage	joker	enjoy	change

Phototeque

unit twenty

Dialogue

DONALD: Ms. Nash, my grandparents visited the United States a few months ago. When they came back, they told us that North Americans celebrate some of the same holidays that we do.

MS. NASH: That's right, Donald. What else did they say?

DONALD: They said, "North American schools have holidays on Christmas and Easter, but the other holidays are different from ours."

MS. NASH: Did they tell you when Christmas and Easter were celebrated?

DONALD: Yes, they said that these two holidays were celebrated in the West on the same days, but that the manner of celebrating them differs in various countries.

MS. NASH: Easter is celebrated in the United States in more or less the same way as it is celebrated in other Western countries. It is a day of rest. People go to church, and the churches have special services.

DONALD: My grandparents said, "Christmas is celebrated differently from the way it is celebrated in Latin American countries." Is this true?

MS. NASH: Yes, it is. In the United States there is usually no celebration like *Nochebuena*. The children go to bed early on Christmas Eve and wait for Santa Claus to come. The next morning they get up early, and there is a Christmas tree in the living room covered with lights and ornaments. Under the tree there are all the toys and presents which Santa Claus has brought for everyone. Later in the day, the family gathers together, and there is a big dinner with roast turkey and other special dishes. This is the traditional

Christmas Day celebration in the United States.

Answer these questions:
1. Where did Donald's grandparents go a few months ago?
2. When they returned, what did they tell their grandchildren?
3. When are Christmas and Easter celebrated? Are they celebrated on the same days in the West?
4. Are these two holidays celebrated in the same way in all Western countries?
5. How is Easter celebrated in your country?
6. How is Christmas celebrated in your country?
7. What is *Nochebuena?*
8. What happens in the United States on Easter?
9. What happens in the United States on Christmas Eve?
10. Describe a traditional Christmas Day in the United States.

Grammar and Usage

Indirect Speech: Statements and Information Questions

a. When the words of a speaker are given exactly or directly as spoken, we call this direct speech. When the words of a speaker are not given exactly as spoken but are given indirectly, we call this indirect speech.

Direct Speech:	She said, "I like to study."
Indirect Speech:	She said that she liked to study.
Direct Speech:	He said to me, "I am busy."
Indirect Speech:	He told me that he was busy.

b. When the form of a sentence is changed from direct to indirect speech, the verb changes from present to past tense. *Tell* is usually used in all indirect sentences when the person to whom the words were spoken is mentioned.

She said to me, "The schools have holidays."
She told *me* that the schools *had* holidays.

c. When direct questions are expressed in indirect speech, the question form is not retained.

He asked, "Where does John work?"
He asked where John worked.

Exercises

A. Change from direct to indirect speech.
   1. He said, "I'm going away." (He said he was going away.)
   2. She said to me, "I don't like holidays."
   3. Grace said, "I hope we have roast turkey for dinner."
   4. Carol said to him, "You'll have to come back later."
   5. The doctor said, "You will have to take this medicine for your cough."
   6. He said, "My vocabulary is not very large."
   7. My mother said to us, "We are going to have dinner early tonight."
   8. My grandparents said, "There are many holidays in the United States."

B. Change from direct to indirect speech.
   1. She asked, "Where does he work?" (She asked where he worked.)
   2. She asked me, "Where does he work?"
   3. They asked us, "When did you arrive?"
   4. I asked him, "Where have you been?"
   5. He asked, "What is *Nochebuena?*"
   6. She asked me, "How do you like my new shoes?"
   7. We asked them, "What time is it?"
   8. He asked the waiter, "What is that bird called?"

C. Change the following questions to indirect form. Use the words in parentheses.
   1. Where is Dave? (I don't know . . .) (I don't know where Dave is.)
   2. Where does she live? (He wants to know . . .)
   3. How much does it cost? (Can you tell me . . .)
   4. What time did they leave? (I'm not sure . . .)
   5. How is he getting along? (His mother wants to know . . .)
   6. Where is the library? (Please tell me . . .)
   7. How often do you exercise? (She wants to know . . .)
   8. How are you? (I want to know . . .)

D. Change from indirect to direct form.
1. He asked me where I lived. (He asked me, "Where do you live?")
2. They said they would not go.
3. She said she could not go.
4. I said I might not go.
5. I told him it was eight o'clock.
6. She said her name was Patricia White.
7. He asked me where I was going.
8. We told them that it was late.

Reading and Conversation:
A French Traveler in England

A Frenchman was once traveling in England. He could speak English quite well but not perfectly. For one thing, his vocabulary was not large.

One day, he was having a meal in a small country hotel and wanted to order some eggs. But he couldn't remember the word for eggs.

Suddenly, through the window, he saw a rooster walking in the yard. He immediately asked the waiter what the bird was called in English.

The waiter told him that it was called a rooster.

The Frenchman then asked what the rooster's wife was called.

The waiter told him that she was called a hen.

The Frenchman then asked what the hen's children were called.

The waiter told him that they were chickens.

The Frenchman then asked what the chickens were called before they were born.

The waiter told him they were called eggs.

"Fine!" said the Frenchman. "Please bring me two eggs and a cup of coffee."

A. Comprehension and Conversation

1. Where was the traveler from? Where was he traveling?
2. How good was his English?
3. Do you have a large English vocabulary? How many words do you think you know in English?

4. What was the traveler trying to order? Where was he?
5. What is a *rooster?* A *hen?* A *chicken?* An *egg?*
6. What do you think of the method the man from France used to order his meal?
7. Do you eat eggs? How do you like them to be prepared?
8. Do you drink coffee? Tea? What other drinks do you enjoy?
9. Do you think the traveler was ordering breakfast, lunch, or dinner? Why?
10. Describe the job of a waiter in a restaurant.

B. Vocabulary

Nouns		*Verbs*	*Adjectives*
Easter	rooster	come back	various
church	chicken	differ	traditional
toy	method	gather	
wife	present	be called	
waiter	service	celebrate	*Adverbs*
hen	celebration		perfectly
Christmas	Santa Claus		quite
manner	Latin America		
lights	ornaments		
dish	roast turkey		

C. Expressions

Use each of these expressions in a sentence.
different from, more or less, gather together, the same way, a day of rest.

D. Pronunciation Drill

tʃ   as in <u>c</u>ello, adven<u>t</u>ure, wa<u>tch</u>

chair	actual	reach
chief	capture	teach
chess	butcher	couch
choice	feature	approach
choose	natural	lunch
cheap	picture	march

unit twenty-one

Dialogue

JAN: Ms. Nash, yesterday we talked about Christmas and Easter. Today, let's talk about some other holidays in the United States.

MS. NASH: There are two in particular which are interesting because they serve as the traditional beginning and end of the summer vacation period for students. Many people celebrate them by going to the seashore or to mountain resorts.

DONALD: I think I know them. My grandparents asked me if I knew them, and I was able to tell them correctly. One of them is Memorial Day, which is observed on the last Monday in May in most states. That is a day to remember the many soldiers who have died in the wars in which the United States took part. The other one is Labor Day, the first Monday in September. That is a day of rest dedicated to the working people of the country.

MS. NASH: Thanksgiving Day is an important holiday in the United States, too. It is celebrated on the fourth Thursday of November. It was first celebrated by the Pilgrims, who were some of the first settlers of the United States.

JAN: What about the Fourth of July? My friend Rick told me that was an important holiday, too.

MS. NASH: He was right. Independence Day is celebrated because the Declaration of Independence was signed on July 4, 1776. That was when the thirteen original colonies separated from England and became an independent country.

MIKE: Are there any holidays which honor specific people in your nation's history?

MS. NASH: Yes, there are. They're not as important as the holidays we've talked about, but they're important, too. There's Martin Luther King, Jr.'s birthday on January 15, Abraham Lincoln's birthday on February 12, George Washington's birthday on February 22, and Columbus Day on October 12. We sometimes celebrate these holidays on a Monday so that we can have a long weekend.

Answer these questions:
1. What are the most important holidays in the United States besides Easter and Christmas?
2. What are the most important national holidays in your country?
3. Who first established the custom of celebrating Thanksgiving Day?
4. What happened on July 4, 1776?
5. What is Memorial Day?
6. To whom is Labor Day dedicated? When is it?
7. Who was Martin Luther King? Christopher Columbus? Abraham Lincoln?
8. Who was the first president of the United States? Who is president today?
9. What two days traditionally serve as the beginning and end of the summer vacation period for students?
10. What is your favorite holiday? Why?

Grammar and Usage

Indirect Speech: Simple Questions and Commands

a. When we change a simple question from direct speech to indirect speech, it is introduced by *if*.

Direct: He asked me, "Do you like my car?"
Indirect: He asked me *if* I liked his car.

b. To express commands in indirect speech, we use the infinitive form of the verb. Note that the subject of the infinitive is in the objective case.

Direct: She said to us, "Come back later!"
Indirect: She told us to come back later.
Direct: I said to them, "Don't do that!"
Indirect: I told them not to do that.

Exercises

A. Change these sentences from direct to indirect form.
   1. She asked me, "Do you intend to see them?" (She asked me if I intended to see them.)
   2. He asked the waiter, "Is that bird called a chicken?"
   3. I asked, "Does she live on State Street?"
   4. I asked, "Is it six o'clock yet?"
   5. We asked the man, "Do you know where we can find a good restaurant?"
   6. They asked us, "Have you read any books by Hemingway?"
   7. You asked her, "Are you a relative?"
   8. She asked him, "Will you come to dinner?"

B. Change these sentences from direct to indirect form.
   1. The teacher said to us, "Wait in this room!" (The teacher told us to wait in this room.)
   2. She said to him, "Don't call me again!"
   3. We said to them, "Bring us a copy of your handwriting."
   4. Ms. Nash said to her students, "Be careful when you write your answers."
   5. I said to her, "Don't make the same mistake again."
   6. My father begged us, "Try to be on time."
   7. He said to me, "Sit down for a minute!"
   8. You said to me, "Tell me the truth about this."

C. Rewrite these sentences first beginning each with *he told me,* then beginning each with *she asked me.*
   1. Come back later. (He told me to come back later. She asked me to come back later.)
   2. Wait in the lobby.
   3. Write it in pencil.
   4. Don't stand there.
   5. Be careful!
   6. Don't lie to me again.
   7. Bring it back immediately.
   8. Take this to Ms. Stone.

D. Change from direct to indirect form. Use contractions.
   1. He said to me, "I'll be back soon." (He told me he'd be back soon.)

2. She asked me, "Where do you live?"
3. She asked me, "Do you live on Tenth Street?"
4. He said to me, "Be sure to write to me."
5. He said, "I don't know."
6. I asked her, "When are you going to return?"
7. She said, "I'm going out of town."
8. I asked her, "Will you get back this week?"

Reading and Conversation:
Balzac as a Student of Handwriting

Honoré de Balzac, the famous French writer, was a man of many accomplishments. In his own opinion, one of his main accomplishments was his ability as a student of handwriting. He had spent much time on this subject, and he often told his friends that he could accurately describe a person's character from a sample of that person's handwriting.

One day, a woman friend brought him a sample of a boy's handwriting. She said that she wanted to know what Balzac thought of the boy's character.

Balzac studied the handwriting carefully for a few minutes. Then he looked at the woman strangely. The woman, however, told him that the boy was no relative of hers and that he could tell her the truth.

"Good!" said Balzac. "Then I can speak frankly." _откровенно_

He then went on to say that he thought the boy was a careless and lazy person. He added that the boy should be watched carefully; otherwise, he would grow up to bring disgrace upon his family.

"Isn't that interesting," said the woman, smiling. "This happens to be a page from a notebook which you yourself used when you were a small boy."

A. Comprehension and Conversation

1. Who was Honoré de Balzac? Do you know any of his writings?
2. What did he consider one of his main accomplishments? Why?
3. What did he think he could know from a person's handwriting?
4. Do you think this is possible? What might someone be able to tell from a sample of your handwriting?

5. What did a woman bring him one day? Why?
6. Why do you think Balzac looked at the woman strangely before he began to talk to her about the boy's handwriting?
7. How did she respond to this look?
8. What did Balzac say about the boy?
9. Describe the surprise ending to this story.
10. How do you think Balzac felt after the woman told him it had been his own handwriting?

B. Vocabulary

Nouns	Verbs	Adjectives
labor	take part	independent
period	dedicate	major
resort	separate	national
war	intend	own
truth	beg	lazy
ability	lie	careless
opinion	add	main
sample	grow up	
accomplishments	bring disgrace	
Thanksgiving	upon	*Adverbs*
Memorial Day		accurately
seashore		frankly
Pilgrim		
birthday		
relative		
handwriting		
character		

C. Expressions

Use each of these expressions in a sentence.
in particular, some of the first, be careful, his own opinion, otherwise.

D. Pronunciation Drill

1 as in lady, follow, well

left	believe	all	tell
leave	hello	girl	silent
little	only	shall	careless
life	belong	will	lip

National Archives

unit twenty-two

Vocabulary

A. Fill in the blanks with the opposites of the following words:

careful	careless	top	_____
clean	_____	false	_____
useless	_____	early	_____
in front of	_____	west	_____
finish	_____	buy	_____
forget	_____	tall	_____
poor	_____	high	_____
below	_____	inside	_____
sad	_____	far	_____
stupid	_____	quickly	_____

B. Give the adverbial form of these adjectives:

recent	recently	frank	_____
immediate	_____	sudden	_____
hard	_____	good	_____
fast	_____	slow	_____
convenient	_____	comfortable	_____

C. Supply the correct preposition.
1. I want to send it by air mail.
2. He makes a lot of mistakes _____ spelling.
3. She was absent _____ class yesterday.
4. He was thinking _____ the sad state _____ Scotland.
5. Peter was deep _____ thought.
6. She was famous _____ the apple trees which she grew.
7. I'll be over to see you _____ Wednesday night.
8. Did you buy a ticket _____ Chicago?
9. It's hard _____ me to get up in the morning.
10. I want to ask you a question _____ your resumé.

D. Fill in the blanks with the correct past and past participle forms of the following verbs:

teach	taught	taught
hurt	_____	_____

cut	_____	_____
dedicate	_____	_____
celebrate	_____	_____
choose	_____	_____
set	_____	_____
fly	_____	_____
lie	_____	_____
admit	_____	_____
break	_____	_____
smoke	_____	_____
count on	_____	_____
get away with	_____	_____
come back	_____	_____
gather	_____	_____
like	_____	_____
enter	_____	_____
taste	_____	_____
lose	_____	_____

E. Use each of these words in a sentence first as a verb, then as a noun: (I _wish_ you a happy birthday. My _wish_ is for a good grade.)

wish	heat	love	hope
smell	help	place	sound
snow	honor	plan	end
rain	look	plant	cheer

F. Use each of these idiomatic expressions in a sentence.
take a walk, be born, get dirty, get away with, by oneself, for a while, word for word, come upon, get off, get on, get up.

G. Underline the correct answer.
1. Which of these animals has the longest neck: elephant, rabbit, bear, <u>giraffe</u>?
2. Which of these does one buy in a post office: peacock, package, stamps, receipt?
3. Which of these is a person with a lot of money: scientist, corporal, waiter, millionaire?
4. Which of these does a spider make: web, cave, trip, receipt?
5. Which of the following holidays was first celebrated by the Pilgrims: Easter, Memorial Day, Labor Day, Thanksgiving?

6. Which of these do people in the United States put on Christmas trees: Santa Claus, ornaments, samples, computers?
7. Which of the following words is not spelled correctly: suddenly, continue, vocabulery, adverbial?
8. The word *trees* is pronounced to rhyme with (this, freeze, piece, pass).
9. The contraction *I'd* is pronounced to rhyme with (need, friend, died, paid).
10. The word *through* is pronounced to rhyme with (true, go, cough, cow).

Grammar

Underline the correct answer.
1. Which of these verbs is in the past tense: break, drive, sent, buy?
2. Which of these verbs is in the present tense: died, agreed, ride, robbed?
3. Which of the following verbs has the same form in the present and past tenses: send, put, take, die?
4. She (told, told us) that she didn't want to go.
5. He said his name (is, was) Robert.
6. Can you drive a car? Yes, I (can/do).
7. My sister can run very (fast, fastly).
8. She can run (quicklier, more quickly) than I can.
9. We all (must, must to) study tonight.
10. If Joe had studied, he (will pass, would have passed).
11. The letter was (write, written) by my friend.
12. He said he (will, would) be back by five o'clock.
13. They came earlier (as, than) we.
14. She asked me where I (lived/live).
15. This work must (finish, be finished) by today.
16. Would you mind (coming, to come) back later?
17. If yesterday (was, had been) a holiday, I'd have gone to the seashore.
18. If I (was, were) you, I wouldn't say anything about it.
19. He said he (must, had to) go to the hospital last night to see a friend.
20. As soon as they (come, have come), I'll tell them.

appendix

The Principal Parts of Irregular Verbs Found in Book 2

Present	Past	Past Participle
be	was/were	been
bear	bore	borne
bet	bet	bet
break	broke	broken
bring	brought	brought
choose	chose	chosen
come	came	come
cost	cost	cost
cut	cut	cut
do	did	done
fall	fell	fallen
find	found	found
forget	forgot	forgotten
get	got	gotten
grow	grew	grown
hang	hung	hung
hide	hid	hidden
hurt	hurt	hurt
lie (recline)	lay	lain
lose	lost	lost
pay	paid	paid
put	put	put
shake	shook	shaken
sit	sat	sat
steal	stole	stolen
take	took	taken
teach	taught	taught
understand	understood	understood

Sample Conjugations

Verb: *to be*

Present Tense
I am	we are
you are	you are
he, she, it is	they are

Past Tense
I was	we were
you were	you were
he was	they were

Future Tense
I will be	we will be
you will be	you will be
he will be	they will be

Present Perfect Tense
I have been	we have been
you have been	you have been
he has been	they have been

Past Perfect Tense
I had been	we had been
you had been	you had been
he had been	they had been

Verb: *to work* (simple form)

ACTIVE VOICE

Present Tense
I work	we work
you work	you work
he, she, it works	they work

Past Tense
I worked	we worked
you worked	you worked
he worked	they worked

Future Tense
I will work	we will work

you will work	you will work
he will work	they will work

Present Perfect Tense

I have worked	we have worked
you have worked	you have worked
he has worked	they have worked

Past Perfect Tense

I had worked	we had worked
you had worked	you had worked
he had worked	they had worked

Verb: *to see*

PASSIVE VOICE

Present Tense

I am seen	we are seen
you are seen	you are seen
he, she, it is seen	they are seen

Past Tense

I was seen	we were seen
you were seen	you were seen
he was seen	they were seen

Future Tense

I will be seen	we will be seen
you will be seen	you will be seen
he will be seen	they will be seen

Present Perfect Tense

I have been seen	we have been seen
you have been seen	you have been seen
he has been seen	they have been seen

Past Perfect Tense

I had been seen	we had been seen
you had been seen	you had been seen
he had been seen	they had been seen

International Phonetic Alphabet

Consonants

[p]—pie, hope, happy

[b]—bell, bite, globe

[f]—fine, office

[v]—vest, of, have

[k]—keep, can, book

[g]—go, get, egg

[l]—let, little, lay

[m]—man, must, dime

[n]—no, down, ton

[ŋ]—sing, ringing

[w]—water, we, one

[θ]—thin, three, path

[ð]—they, then, other

[s]—see, sat, city

[z]—zoo, does, is

[ʃ]—shoe, ship, action

[ʒ]—usual, garage

[tʃ]—chance, watch

[dʒ]—June, edge

[r]—red, rich, write

[y]—you, yes, million

[h]—he, hat, who

[t]—ten, to, meet

[d]—do, did, sudden

Vowels and Diphthongs

[ɪ]—it, did, build

[i]—me, see, people

[ɛ]—end, let, any

[æ]—cat, bat, laugh

[ɑ]—army, father, hot

[ɔ]—all, caught, long

[ʊ]—book, full, took

[u]—too, move, fruit

[ə]—cup, soda, infant

[ɚ]—her, work, bird

[e]—say, they, mail

[o]—old, coal, sew

[aɪ]—dry, eye, buy

[ɔɪ]—toy, boy, soil

[aʊ]—cow, our, house

NOTE: In accordance with common practice and for reasons of simplification, these minor changes in symbols have been introduced. [ə] and [ɚ] are used in this book for both stressed and unstressed syllables. [y] is used instead of IPA [j]. [ɑ] is used instead of IPA [a].